AF397418

JONATHAN E

# It's a Sin...?

## All in the name of love!

novum pro

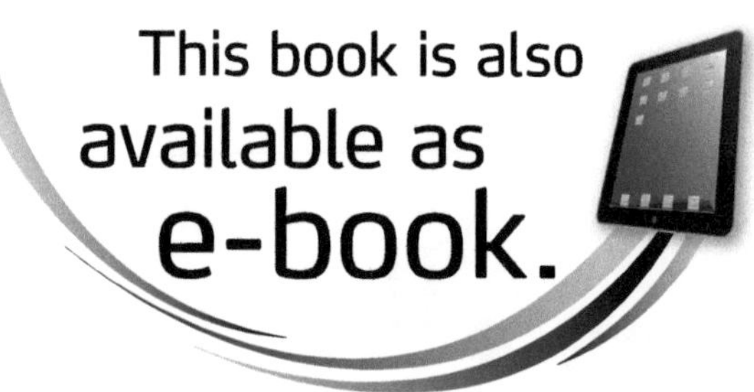

© 2022 novum publishing

ISBN 978-3-99131-400-4
Editing: Ashleigh Brassfield, DipEdit
Cover photo:
Rdonar | Dreamstime.com
Cover design, layout & typesetting:
novum publishing

www.novum-publishing.co.uk

# Contents

# Preface

Since time immemorial, human nature, being what it is and always will be, gives rise to an inner desire to share one's life with another person. To create a bond between two people, experience the warmth, comfort, and mutual love of being able to share life's events with someone, is in built in each of our DNA.

Whether that bond is between male/female, male/male, female/female – human nature drives each of us to seek that one special person.

Whilst our individual DNA is fixed, are there external events/factors that impact, and possibly change, the course of our life's journey?

What impact have religion, societal expectations, and family traditions on one's behaviour and attitude? Do the law and respective legal systems that govern one's country of residence have an impact?

How have world events (First and Second World Wars), innovations (enabling global travel), and technology (for example, giving rise to social media) impacted one's life journey and whom each of us choose to share it with?

January 2020 triggered events that certainly impacted each of us: Tim included!

It was June 2020: the impact of the global pandemic appeared to be easing, and one was able to start exploring outside after several months of being told to "stay at home." Finally, Tim could go for a walk in the local park. After walking alone for some thirty minutes, Tim decided it was time for a coffee and saw, a short distance in front of him, that the local café was finally open, with table & chairs set up on the external decking area. Tim found a quiet spot in the corner.

Whilst enjoying his coffee, Tim looked over to the grass area, where many were enjoying the sunshine. *How times have changed,* Tim thought to himself. From what he could see and hear, there were many nationalities; some wearing summer clothes comprising of just shorts & T shirt, others in long trousers or dresses, the occasional person wearing a suit but no tie. At the end of the park, a football game was in progress. There was lots of hugging between the players. Lifting each other congratulatory, close enough to be personal contact without the kiss on the cheek. This 'on the pitch' behaviour was accepted by all.

Tim, looking in the opposite direction, then noticed two young guys walking hand in hand, wearing very tight shorts, one of them bare-chested. They were totally engrossed in their conversation and seemed extremely happy.

As Tim continued to watch the two guys, the scene triggered memories of his youth, albeit more than 60 years ago, and he started to make comparisons. Overall, Tim thought he hadn't done to bad. He had always worked, at one point owned his own business; eventually owned a car and his home. Tim's journey through life is by no means unique. However, his lifestyle certainly was impacted by religion, societal expectations, family traditions and world events!

The following chapters recall Tim's life experiences in searching for, finding, and losing that fundamental human gift, when born into this world: that of the inner desire to experience love, to be loved, to share love and, ultimately, to lose love.

This book is dedicated to:

- All whose lives have been cut short as a result of "Society", world events, peer pressure.
- All who challenged "The Law" and fought for human nature to be freely expressed and enable the human right to follow one's inner self and experience that immortal desire of love, to be loved, to share love and to give love.
- All who are reading this book at the time of questioning one's sexuality and asking oneself, "Is it a Sin?"
- All who are questioning whether the changes in society, the law, and technology resulted in a positive outcome?

# CHAPTER 1

# 1930s: The Great Depression & Teenage Years

Tim was born in June 1934. His father, William, was a senior clerk with the local council. Martha, Tim's mum, worked part time cleaning & cooking at the Village Manor, whilst at the same time looking after 7 children.

William & Martha had lived locally all their lives; childhood sweethearts, they married in their local Catholic church in their late teens. Home was a three-bedroom terraced house, one of thirty houses located on each side of a long and narrow cobbled street. William's eight brothers and sisters, along with a similar number of Martha's family, all lived within five miles of each other; a very close-knit community environment.

One may say Tim's arrival was an accident, with his youngest sister at the time, Mavis, being 12, and his four other siblings aged 14 to 22; two sisters and three brothers in total. Birth control was virtually non-existent and abortion never an option … never permitted to even be discussed. When Tim was seven, a baby sister was born.

## Leaving School and Meeting Expectations

Once one reached the age of 14 schooling ended, and one was expected to find work or join the Army, Navy or Airforce in order to contribute to family finances. Hence, during Tim's younger years he did not see much of his brothers and sisters apart from Mavis, twelve years older than Tim. Tim's eldest brother, Walter, was in the Air Force, stationed in what was then known as Southern Rhodesia (now Zimbabwe). Harold, the next eldest brother, was a sailor serving on board the destroyer HMS Howe.

Tim recalls his early years comprised of spending a considerable amount of time with Mavis, joining in her games; playing with her dollhouse and dressing her dolls with brightly coloured clothes and materials. As time would tell, later in life, this early introduction to dressing up/being creative & 'arty' influenced Tim's future activities, both at work and for pleasure.

The long street resulted in many children also playing in the street. Innovation and technology had only extended to the occasional household owning a small wireless (radio), and no child had the joy of watching television nor using modern technology. This resulted in creating their own games and pastimes from their own ingenuity and a sense of curiosity, creating endless hours of enjoyment for virtually no cost.

## Little Contact with Dad & Brothers

Tim saw very little of his father. On Saturdays Tim's father would go to the local football/cricket match, along with, when possible, two of Tim's older brothers who, like their father, loved all sports; it was a big part of their life. Walter, the eldest brother, who like Tim was not sporty, would be working down the pit. The local coal mines, being a large employer in the area, also employed three of Tim's uncles. That was until WW2 broke out, when any male 18 and over was enlisted.

Sunday lunch time, Tim's father would join Tim's five uncles at the Hare & Hounds for their customary pre-Sunday-lunch drinks. One of Tim's uncles was captain of the Hare & Hounds dart team. The team's practice and dart matches typically consumed three, if not four nights a week for Tim's father & uncles. On top of this, Tim's father and uncles would spend time attending boxing matches, watching his brothers compete, and going to the horse & dog races.

Throughout the family the subject of sport was laboured, particularly on his father's side: boxers and footballers, some of them of note. All his uncles had been involved in it, as far as history told.

Seeing very little of his father, Tim was very close to his mum. This continued to be the case for the remainder of Tim's school years.

Academically, Tim was always in the top ten of his year; however, he had just a few friends at school.

## Not Being Part of the Team

Tim had never been a sportsman, or indeed, a lover of any sport in general. He would do anything to avoid the one subject he disliked most – as time would prove!

Like lots of boys his age, Tim didn't quite understand that to be a boy, he had to "be on the team," so to speak. When it came to PE lessons the teacher encouraged competition and would create four teams. Each team had a team leader, and they would take it in turns to choose which boys would be in their teams. One could not describe Tim as being large-built, but he certainly was not the thinnest or fittest, and not being sports-minded, was always nearly the last, if not the last, to be asked to join a team. This sense of rejection continued to play on Tim's mind and made him feel different, or even abnormal.

Tim also found himself on the receiving end of schoolboy bullying. One particular boy, in the next year above Tim, would make him share whatever Tim's mum had packed for lunch. Tim had learnt that failure to comply would result in receiving a beating.

Overall, Tim's self-confidence was not his strength and, again, played on Tim's mind.

# Being Close to Mum – Consequences

Tim also recalls, upon reflection, the verbal bullying in his early years. The saying "tied to his mother's apron strings" was common in those days; boys who behaved in that way were referred to as "loners." At the time Tim did not know any different. Tim had his hobbies and occasionally went out and about with his few friends; he wasn't an unhappy child.

Like all children from big families, Tim was used to family squabbles, perhaps more so, as his two older brothers had been in the armed forces and abroad for so many of his growing years. The family disputes were usually late at night, for whatever reason. Walter, Tim's eldest brother, more than 20 years older, had obviously seen more of life and its experiences than Tim.

Whatever the reason for the latest argument, Tim's eldest brother was obviously aware of the closeness between his mother and his younger brother.

Tim's memories often took him back to the hours when the two of them had left the family home mid-argument and walked the streets, whatever the weather, until things had quietened down. They would wait in the outside toilet until everyone had gone to bed.

Tim had one outstanding memory of all these times, but he never understood it. That memory was of Walter pointing at Tim holding onto his mother, shouting, "He's queer!" "Look at him, queer!" Looking back now, it is easy to realise why the subject was never discussed.

The two brothers really never got on, there was always friction, but many years later things might have changed as life itself changed.

It is strange to think that as life became more normal to Tim and he met so many guys like himself, guys from different backgrounds, occupations, etc., it was difficult to realise these were the times of the illegality for them all, irrespective of who they were. Knowing so many people who would introduce Tim to "my twin brother," "my younger brother," or sometimes older, in a genuine loving way; perhaps this is why Tim could not understand his own situation.

## Displaying Artistic Skills

It is a known fact that many homosexuals are, to a great extent, part of the "arty world," and Tim has many memories of his involvement with that side of life.

Brothers who would have shared a life in the theatre world – not necessarily on stage but, in one case, one of them was in the orchestra, a brilliant pianist, and the other the musical director. Both were super guys in their own right, but very respectable and discreet. It may be remembered that one so-called 'star of stage and screen' sought to discover why he was gay and yet not his brother; consequent programs gave reasons, but were they undeniably correct or was it hope? It has to be remembered that although this was many years ago, before the 1967 changes in the sexuality act being passed, it was also not too distant from the Second World War, and all children had come through an experience they didn't understand.

## "Wartime" Childhood and Schooling

Children were either rough and ready, due to the times, or delicate; both self-explanatory. It is easy to understand that they were rough and ready, not in presentation, but because of the shortages and rationing. Family standards had, perhaps reluctantly, suffered, and the children behaved as best as they knew: well behaved, polite, and well cared-for, but all around them the ruins of buildings and houses they were familiar with, still standing derelict, awaiting demolition or some other such fate, changing all around them.

Of course, those referred to as delicate were the children who, apart from sharing all of that, needed the closeness of parents, family etc. So many had been torn away from such safety into being evacuees, taken at a minute's notice from all that was familiar to be placed in unusual circumstances – frightening, to say the least. It wasn't necessarily health conditions that made those boys and girls delicate; it was what was going on around them that made them clingy. No, it did not make them homosexual, as is sometimes suggested; they were genuinely more sensitive than others in many ways. One mentions this simply because, after a night like Tim had spent – and by no means was he alone in this – the children then had to face a day of schooling, although it can be said that that in itself was not as gruelling as we may think today's education program is. The formalities were different. There was always the morning milk to look forward to, not to mention the track home to lunch and back again. But we needed to learn, and we did so in the simplest of forms.

There was no school bus, no uniform regulations, but in the conditions of the day we were taught well.

Often through shortages of teachers and equipment, children of the era were brought up totally different to the modern generation, which is to be expected. There was no technology, for instance. Our play time was all self-initiated, with the simplest of items to turn into playthings, and sex education lessons, as such, were not discussed.

Maybe this simple lifestyle gave us a good foundation to life itself, for this generation of prospective gays turned out to be respectable citizens of society and the lack of is easy to see in this modern free-for-all world.

Tim's family was an ordinary working-class family. Mum had brought up the family, just as all mothers did in the days of his youth. There were none of what we would call luxuries: washing machines, fridges, etc. Radios were called 'wireless' and the probable luxury was having, in the latter part of his growing up, a radiogram on which vinyl records could be played to provide a little light entertainment.

We should think about the comparisons of wages, then and now. Tim has noticed in these declining years that people, some anyhow, are always eager to compare life then with what are called modern times.

## Community Spirit – Yes, It Did Exist

There was an air of everyone making an effort, to help themselves and each other. Of course, there were people who were a little better off than their neighbours, but they never made a show of it.

Perhaps the couple next door had one child, a nice home that suited their needs, but neighbours were not envious of each other. It was more likely they would go out of their way to help each other.

It wasn't unknown, especially in area such as where Tim lived, that one family of several children would help another in the same bracket by handing down clothes if there were children of a similar age. Bear in mind there were no such things as charity shops.

One might imagine these children being the butt of jokes, but that wasn't the case. A shirt, a jumper, whatever could be dyed and represented next day without shame, ironed, pressed … who knew? Today, it's probably a case of "what's a dye?"

They were not the dark days, as so often referred to; the simplest of tasks were shared, tasks that cost little or no money.

The scrubbing of doorsteps, a weekly job for most, sweeping outside the front of one's home … Do your own, do the neighbours too, whilst you're on your hands and knees! Out would come the bucket of water scrubbing brush, the carbolic soap and the white powder that made the step look as though it had never been trodden on!

One can almost hear the words of a modern generation … "I would have let them do their own!" Yes! Because that's how times have changed, changed in the simplest of ways, not always for the better.

However, Tim was happy living at home with his brothers &
sisters, and this may sound contradictory to Tim's previous references to his older brother, but one by one, they did marry and
leave home.

# CHAPTER 2

# 1940s: WW2

## No Mod-Cons, Just Elbow Grease and Long Hours

Tim recalls that when he was growing up household chores were all manual and using the "equipment" of the day, that was fashionable; a dolly tub, a hand driven wringer, and washday was made a little easier. If you were extremely lucky a vacuum cleaner (hoover) was an asset, but mostly the housework was done on a routine basis, with all hands to the pumps, so to speak. Everyone helped, and it was not unusual for mum to also go out to work, for a myriad of reasons. Although it was very necessary, they did not all find secretarial work. Mums were known to have had to work the strangest of hours, not always suitable when trying to raise a family, but it was a case of just having to in order to ensure there was food on the table and clothes for the children to wear. For example, bus and tram conductors and post women, who had replaced the local postman as all males were called to war, would find their working days would start at two or three in the morning and continue until the late delivery at 17:00. All this so they could try to afford the "extras" needed at home.

Young men being called up for service often meant a change in finances to families, so it was important, no, essential the woman, in addition to being housewife and mother, also go out to work, more often than not juggling more than one job.

## Financial Prudence Learnt at an Early Age

For Tim, like his parents and grandparents, it had always been a point of pride to declare, "If you can't afford it, don't have it." However, the impact of bringing up a family whilst Dad, brother, uncles and nephews were 'serving their country', meant it was often the only way that what were considered 'luxuries', but in reality necessities, could be obtained.

Hire purchase was the only way some could afford the things they needed. There was no such thing as credit cards; strict enquiries were made as to the capability of being able to pay and, as Tim found out many years later when working in a furniture store, it was always important to protect the customer and the trader.

It's true people were afraid to enter into such agreements, but it was not easy as today. Tim remembers, all too well, the embarrassment of having to tell a customer they could not make a purchase as they still owed £1 on the last item they had bought … How times have changed, both in terms of the attitude towards buying on credit and the readily available range of credit cards that are so freely pushed by banks/financial institutions in today's accepted culture of "buy now – pay later."


## War Time – Evacuation

Like many other children, Tim was evacuated for a while during the war years; he was lucky in as much as he had his two sisters and a brother with him.

To live in the country and go to school there was a way of life he could never have imagined, but he was, or rather they were, unfortunate in that the folk they lived with were not as kind as perhaps they could, or should, have been. However, it was only two hours from home, so their parents could visit by bus, often bringing with them toys and goodies they were deprived of.

Still, it was nice when the time came to return home to parents and familiarity. His two older brothers had been called for military service, as was the law of the time.


## Brotherly Connections

Tim's brothers and sisters had been brought up to go to Sunday school, although it seemed different in the country; they were happy to be back in places they knew with familiar people.

In these memories, Tim has spoken of having three brothers and three sisters. Like all families, they generally got on well together, as siblings do in their varying ways. The tale of his eldest brother's relationship with him has taken up enough space; his second eldest brother was more understanding, as you will see – maybe him having served in the navy explains some of that. He seemed to understand Tim better, and the third brother, who was not only closer in age but in other ways too. Looking back, this one seemed to understand on an intimate level and as he grew older, Tim could remember things his brother had said which fitted in with Tim's lifestyle. Tim's third brother was sensitive and caring too, and throughout his life had always made it known how proud of Tim he was, and his capabilities with hobbies and interests had been noticed. Tim married a woman who was totally different from himself, and always seemed to put his brother before her.

At some late stage in his life, Tim had reason to wonder about his sexuality, and it was said that perhaps that was the reason for his adoration of his younger brother; maybe he envied him for being so openly gay instead of covering it up, as was the case in those days. He never approached Tim in any other way than brotherly, so perhaps folk were right in their assumptions.

This brother had served his National Service in Germany for eighteen months, but on demobilisation seemed to settle to a quiet life with his own interests and work until meeting his wife.

## The Local "Bobby" – Everyone's Friend – But One Every Child Feared

Tim's dad would tell tales of the policeman that had always been a part of the community. Feared? Respected? What would be the best word to use? The local policeman (or local bobby, as he was affectionally referred to) signified all that is right and good. Tim recalls, whilst growing up, if caught doing anything wrong being frog marched to the local nick, as it was called in those days, by that burly policeman for all to see and witness the shame of those who had done wrong. There was no car readily available to take them to the police station; they were publicly shamed before they arrived there.

Tim's dad and his family lived quite near to the local nick (police station) and, together with his brothers and sisters, would watch the bad boy of the day being taken by the scruff of his neck to face his punishment. Not a nice sight to see, but it brought results! It certainly gave the Bad Boys something to think about and instilled the right idea and attitude into the young men it was meant for but, and it's a BIG but, it also happened to queers of the day, who were quite frequent in public toilets (more on this subject later).

As mentioned earlier, Tim was fond of his dad; he was firm but gentle and, although he had four sons, never showed violence towards them, whatever their misdemeanours. Holidays were not a part of family life – he was not able to afford them – but there were always trips to the seaside on bank holidays, not too far away, and if spare money was in short supply there was always the bus network, which would take them to places which in those days, as kids, we thought were miles away. But in more recent years, Tim has lived in some of those places, which sounds "extra ordinary."

Recalling his life now, Tim knows himself that as he was growing up, leaving school to find work, there was nothing that he could ever imagine was happening to make him think of those times during his childhood years.

# Working Life Begins

Tim worked in shops for many of his early working days, although all the hours were not 9 till 6, but 8 till 5:40, or 8:45 until 6, so that Tim would be there in time to sweep the shop front, page and wash the outside area, and be ready for the first customers when the doors opened for business. Whatever has happened to those nice things that happened without fuss today?

As Tim prepared himself to start the daily shop opening, he hardly believed the filth and rubbish left there for the local council cleaners to do their job. An example of the aggression of mankind in the 20th century may reflect so readily leaving home to be married and start their own lives away from the family. Yes, it was easy in those days to leave a job on Friday night and start a new one on Monday morning without a problem, and Tim, like all youngsters, did this many times. At one time, whilst working in a large furniture store, Tim's job would entail bringing in the exhibits from outside the shop in readiness for closing time. Prior to this Tim had worked in a shop just around the corner. On several occasions a customer from there, Fred, who had always been friendly towards Tim, just happened to get off the train at the same time as Tim on his way home from work. Friendly exchange of hello was usually sufficient, and Fred went on his way home, where his mum was waiting with dinner. Fred was probably 20 years older than Tim and in conversation had mentioned he worked in a newspaper office. Fred was tall, smart, and on occasions would bring a box of Quality Street chocolates whilst venturing to inviting Tim to dinner. It was never accepted, but left Tim bewildered when Fred told him he loved him.

# CHAPTER 3

# 1950s: National Service

## National Service – The End of a Friendship

National service called Tim in 1951 and Tim and Fred never saw each other again. Here, perhaps is an instance of an older man …

Tim remembers and wonders if the times talked about were a reflection on this attraction. Tim remembers Fred for his kindliness, his gentle actions of shaking hands when they met and yes, the chocolates too. In today's world it might be called grooming, but one instantly tries to compare. It could be said it was an incorrect way to behave, one not recognised by Tim himself but remembered for the discreet & gentle way Fred behaved. Maybe the answer is, in many ways, connected with today's living and the aggression found in many things, where in those days trust was more prominent, the norm, simply taken for granted, or possibly more correctly described as expected.

A box of chocolates, which seems suspicious, perhaps, with the filth and squalor, drink and drugs of today; the approach is so different.

In his own army career, Tim chose to follow in the same branch of the army as his brother, Albert, albeit a different country and differing opportunities. By this time the length of service had increased to two years.

## National Service – Leaving Home and the Journey Ahead

Tim was like all lads, not really looking forward to leaving home, but prepared himself as best he could.

Tim thought the hardest thing was when his mother told him, just days before, "I won't come to the station with you, I am going out for the day with Auntie Grace, but you'll be ok, there will be lots of lads on their own." It really was a shock to Tim; he fully expected Mum to come and see him off. It was only years later that Tim realised she had made the best decision for them both.

## National Service – Visiting Mum & Dad

During the initial training, Tim was fortunate to occasionally be able to travel back home for weekends. For Tim's parents it was simply part of their Sunday evening out to have a drink, as was *the* thing to do in those days.

One Sunday, while Tim was waiting at the bus station, to return to camp, his dad said, "Come in and have a drink with us." Tim shuddered at the thought and said no thanks, but his dad said, "It won't hurt you, it's a nice drink," and Tim found himself all dressed up in uniform, holding a port and lemon; the only one ever, but Tim enjoyed it and the memory of having a drink with his dad.

## National Service – Initial Training

That training lasted just 6 months and all of Tim's intake, as it was called, were taken on the first part of their journey abroad.

It really had not been too much of an ordeal completing this training; maybe he settled in rather well, being among strangers and listening to some of their tales of life and, probably because you had to, they just got on with mixing with each other. After all, he was a stranger to some of the things they talked about, and this was life history in the raw. You heard about their working lives, their careers, and their love lives, which they were anxious to talk about, often, for Tim, in too much detail.

Every day was different, new things to learn, new instructors to come face-to-face with, some decent old soldiers who understood with what you were going through and then, on balance, some who had the reputation for being the devil himself. They each had their own favourites and would give an extra helping hand if they thought you needed it.

Because they were in catering training, it helped if you were interested in the subject. So many of these lads, who had never boiled an egg before in their lives, had ambitions to open a Michelin star restaurant after cooking their first fairy cake! … god knows if they did or not, but it certainly helped them to understand how to look after themselves in another dimension.

## National Service Training – The Drill Corporal

Participating in National Service training, Tim was fascinated by the drill corporal, who always manage to call Tim's name in a way Tim hadn't heard before. They got on well and there was a bit of leg pulling, as Tim sees it today, but the Corporal lived in married quarters with his wife and there were celebrations when his wife gave birth to their first child. Just another episode that leaves Tim wondering!

On a human link, there was, on more than one occasion in 6 months when Private "Blogs" would be sent for by the commanding officer, and suddenly dispatched home on compassionate leave, only to return a week later announcing his girlfriend was pregnant and he had to get married by special license. He would suffer the jokes of the Billet, but then everyone waited for the letter to say he was a dad and buy him a pint … how times change.

Billet living was difficult for many young boys; leaving home, being among strangers 24 hours a day. Young men from all different areas of life, different backgrounds, some leaving behind girlfriends, and yes, brides-to-be, often sooner than they imagined, and even a few married men. There were a few married men, of course there were, some who never talked about or even mentioned very little of their lives. Like Tim, it was a life different to anything any of them knew … some more so than others.

## National Service – Tim Encounters His First Admirer

Usually, morning inspection parade was also the time for duty delegation and one guy, it turned out, had been a chef prior to his call up and was always selected for the important jobs–duties. When asked if he wanted a helpmate he would nominate Tim; they worked well together, and so Tim thought nothing of it when his mate pulled his leg amidst comments such as "he fancies you" or "you know what he's after, Tim, don't you?" Tim did not, and thought nothing of it when his colleague put his arm around him, calling him darling, or even when he apologized for squeezing past with the words "sorry, darling." … Tim really didn't realise anything untoward … they were working together, what could be wrong? He accepted it without embarrassment … this was the naive 1950s, after all.

## National Service – Sailing to 1st Assignment – In Hong Kong

Of course, the traveling, and the mode of travel in itself, were a wonderful experience for most of them; rail, planes, and for many more, the experience of a troop ship sailing the high seas, sometimes for weeks on end, as in this case.

It was shared accommodation and shared at very close quarters. There were no luxuries, simply hammocks hung from post to post where possible. Privacy was a word not recognised, and if you had never suffered embarrassment about your body and its parts before, now was the time to get used to it. It was all done in good fun and had to be; if for no other reason, it was the regulations.

It wasn't as if they had all come from the same place. There were soldiers, sailors, and airmen of all nations, all colours, some bronze from lying on the deck, others who treated their bodies like temples. Some big, some smaller, and some even bigger, but they all gathered as groups and enjoyed the experience best they could, until the next port, when names were called and friends said their farewells.

For Tim, and of course, others like him, the experience was all the more fascinating, for in his curiosity he found what some of the other groups were about when he discovered the ship's crew were allowed to spend their free time with the lads on deck.

## National Service – Meeting Mama & Patsy

In particular, two of the guys known as Mama and Patsy putting on their makeup, wigs, and bikinis to sit among them, calling each other female names seemed to be nothing unusual amongst their own kind. They were almost like a variety act, but this was them in their free time.

The boys enjoyed being with them and they liked the boys' company – of course they did. Maybe some of them knew more than they did, but nothing ever happened that wasn't supposed to … remember, man's attraction to man, at this time, was illegal or it seemed "not to have happened."

Tim had never seen anything like this before, it seemed so strange, but others obviously had and enjoyed the fun. There were just "two of them"! This first experience of a "drag" act may have influenced Tim, later in life, as you may discover in a later chapter.

Relaxing in the hot sun, or after showering frequently because of the intense heat, they were to be found lying on their beds naked or with the briefest of covering, and joking about the things guys joke about at times like this … This was their time and they enjoyed it, all lads together. They spoke of home and family.


## National Service – Another Admirer


Ray, the eldest of them, all of 28 years of age, would often joke with Tim, pulling his leg about Tim's naivety on his way of life, no girlfriends etc. It always passed as a joke until one day two of the other guys came back early and saw Ray and Tim sitting on the lower bunk bed together. They warned Ray to be careful and explained to Tim it was not a good idea for them to be found together so close. They all laughed about it and there was never another incident of that kind.

Of course, all this was in the 1950s, and the seriousness of the time is realised in memories, although there were these fears, and even knowledge of such things being part of a world Tim knew so little of.

Looking back at these times, Tim has to admit, as he puts it, that there were some 'stirrings' within him, but he wasn't aware why … so it never became a part of his life. The Chef, in Tim's early days of training, holding Tim close as he passed by, "just so that I can get by, darling," and how far would Ray have been tempted to go if the situation had been different? For Ray was always talking about his girlfriend back home!

## National Service – A New Officer –
## Tim Remains Unaware & Innocent

Tim's colleagues, who shared the billet with him, were often annoyed after a new officer joined the unit. One such new officer (looking back now a proper "camp queen"), who went into town most nights, would arrive back in the billet, sometime later than midnight, and call out loudly for "Mr Tim" (his surname never mentioned) to "Come out and cook supper for my friends, just something simple, curried eggs or ham and chips, something nice to end the evening," –though, by this time, it was near enough breakfast time.

Perhaps the times this new officer called to discuss menus with Tim, usually with a small towel attempting to cover at least some of himself, Tim remembers he did try and peek, and sometimes saw more than he bargained for!

So, it must be true, it's always have been there … the inquisitiveness … and lies dormant until the right moment. Remember, Tim was ignorant, or possibly one may say innocent, at this time. Not alone, one feels, is the right thing to say here.

## National Service – Turning Boys into Men –
## Ready to Defend Their Country

Although it was an experience that none could have imagined, it was, in itself, a teaching and learning period – many young men's "basic training" of life. These boys who had been quiet, shy, soon realised that the training they received was beneficial in many ways. Coming from all backgrounds, they learnt the importance of discipline in their lives and the need to present themselves well. The old jokes they had learned from their fathers, about spit and polish, soon became a reality to them and a big part of the disciplinary teachings that set them on the right tracks for good living, which has surely been reflected in their lives since.

The much feared and besmeared Sergeant Major was in most cases a genuinely ordinary, everyday guy who had made the Army, the Navy, or the Air Force his career. It was part of his makeup to be able to shout his way around the parade ground, no "namby pambies" here – the Sergeant Major has to be seen to be in charge. It will often be said by those in the know that there was no bullying. If a senior NCO was aware of a weakling in his squad, he would make sure he was as strong as the rest, but this would be done in a discreet way. Let it not be forgotten that they who were, or appeared to be, "a bit different" also reached high achievements in their lives. It was only the times they were living in that made it difficult for them, but easy for the bigots.

Tim himself was no different from his mates; he was lucky to find himself in such good company, for now he knows, and has done for many years, that the lads knew more about him than he knew himself … But he regrets nothing.

There's many an adolescent young man in the world today who would benefit from those years; there would probably be less of the aggression on the streets today, and the homosexual guy would find life so much easier to contend with.

So many of the young men who are now finding themselves in this position found it strange, and that was only to be expected. Mama would always have been around to wash clothes and make sure her children were turned out well presented and display a certain standard of good upbringing, but now the lads were doing it for themselves.

Tim recalled a conversation he had in recent times with a young man who questioned the necessity of the national service days and had compared it to being like pretending to be soldiers. For those many thousands who did serve, they will tell you that the training was as real as it could be. One has to remember that these *were* the soldiers, in the event of war, who would be sent to regiments whose very name frightens you. The manoeuvres, the guns, and the weapon training were not pretence; everything was so real. The attempts to bring back National Service still continue, and so they should, for National Service made men out of boys.

It was an age and era which so many young men took part in, not by choice, but because it was law. Of course, it sometimes held opportunities beyond the lads' wildest dreams and a nobody could become a somebody; firstly with a simple stripe on your shoulder, and then progressing through the ranks.

## National Service – First Posting – Arriving in Hong Kong

At the end of 28 days at sea, it was time to be sent to their different units. Tim found himself sent to a small unit manned mainly by young Asian soldiers with a small number of officers and British NCOs, the latter sharing a small billet for the half dozen of them. They were friendly, considerate, and soon made Tim welcome in their group. They all had fun and laughed together, in their off-duty moments.

Tim recalls with pride his arrival in Hong Kong, despite his fears, and those of many of his mates aboard, of being shipped to the Far East to serve in the war that was gaining momentum at that time. Here he was being shown into the commanding officer's office, about to be told he was being posted to a unit in what was then known as "The New Territories" and promoted to corporal to take charge of the catering facilities for a unit in which there were few motorized vehicles, and horses and mules were the main source of transport. Tim had never been in this environment before. On his way out of the office Tim heard what he thought was his name being called, and as he turned, he saw a guy who was the son of his mother's friend. Tim embraced him and gave thanks he wasn't alone in this strange country after all. They were able to visit each other's units and kept up their friendship until his friend married.

## National Service – Communications from Back Home in the UK

It wasn't long after Tim's arrival in Hong Kong, so many miles from home and its familiarity, that he started to receive letters from an old school friend. She had got Tim's address from Tim's mother and wanted to be a pen pal. Tim obliged, although at the time he was not aware of the consequences awaiting on his return to the UK.

## National Service – Social Club Creation

Being in charge of catering, and with his buddies' welfare at heart, Tim was able to convert a disused clubhouse into a plush club where all the guys on the camp could socialize, regardless of nationality (Chinese and English), and they all enjoyed many memorable times away from normal duties.

## National Service – Posting to Hong Kong – Very Happy Memories

What a joy it was, many years later, after Tim had completed his National Service, for him to see new neighbours moving into the house opposite his own who turned out to be Chinese! They had lots to talk about and Tim was able to reminisce on his time in Hong Kong.

Parents, in their mid-40s and two sons of school age – there was much to discuss, and it helped Tim to realise what a privilege it had been, not only to visit their homeland while serving his country, but also to have been able to experience the progress of Hong Kong itself.

They talked of buildings which were in construction whilst Tim was there, and of the simple ways in which this was done compared to what had happened and changed in the country since Tim's return to the UK. It was almost as if the time and memories they shared were, for a nineteen-year-old, an unimaginably long period.


## National Service – Society Attitude – Taboo Subjects Remain

It couldn't be assumed Tim was alone in his in innocence or ignorance, call it what you will; there must have been many hundreds of young men who were called up and were totally unaware on the matters of sexuality. It's different for today's generations to try and imagine that the subject was not discussed. There can be no doubt that there were those who knew it all, by one means or another, but very few parents talked openly about sexuality. It was very much a "nudge nudge, wink wink" subject. But they say, don't they, that where ignorance is bliss it's a folly to be wise? We, the old ones, have grown up with some decency and standards and wonder what is to be gained by being so "out", today, as the saying goes.

In today's world, parents can be heard swearing at, and in front of, the youngest of children; of course, it's not clever and it certainly doesn't attract people to you – well, it does, the lower grade members of society. Alcohol, drugs, and unemployment can all be blamed … But do we not have a craving to better ourselves?

Never hearing bad language from parents wasn't unusual and so moving into the world we never embarrassed ourselves by living in these downtrodden circles. You might think that joining the forces and sharing living quarters with thirty or so other guys would have been an open free for all with regard to sexual conversations, bad language etc., but, never once, Tim will say, was this the case, maybe because of the prevailing laws. Men and women were aware of such conversations and were discreet.

Lads today joining the forces, either on a voluntary basis or in the unlikely event of national conscription becoming law once again, with foul mouths, bad language, and knowledge of sexual matters would not be able to comprehend the privacy the men of years ago lived under. It's easy to acknowledge that times have changed, and to a greater extent secrecy is no longer important, nor are they sure of the privacy desired by so many. If nothing else, we learned during our time of National Service to respect each other.

## National Service – Intolerance and the Impact Thereof

History cannot be changed, we know that for certain, but those of us who are gay now know how lucky we are to have come through unscathed and give thanks for that. But even in this new century there are those still alive, living a decent life in whatever they choose, still carrying a blemish on their character for simply being gay; both men and women dismissed from service with disgrace, and still facing fighting for justice fifty years on.

Whatever sex, male or female, so many were kicked out of the forces for simply being so and living with a criminal record, robbed of their lives, their careers and defrauded of their pension rights, awaiting a royal pardon from the country they were proud to serve and, yes, possibly die for.

Will they, can they, the young people of today, gay & searching, living with mistakes, show respect to these victims by behaving in a way that makes these under souls, who lost their lives simply for being queer, and let us not forget the vile word used, proud.

They were quiet, discreet, often by necessity. Pride may be a modern word; let the more modern important campaign with pride be in our hearts, but however old or young we are, we are remembering Tim and many of his contemporaries.

# CHAPTER 4

# 1960s: Societal Expectations

## Demobilization – A New Relationship – But!

You may recall the pen pal "relationship" Tim had pursued whilst serving National Service in Hong HK. They continued to write to each other and on his return, met up and started to see each other as though it was all so natural; they became engaged. A friend of Tim's had a new newsagent shop built and wanted Tim to manage it, being on a new housing estate with accommodation. It was a very good prospect for Tim on his demobilization from the army.

## Demobilization – Following Society's Expectations – No Choice?

In those days courting, as it was called, was just that; intimacy, sex was not discussed, or at least that was what Tim understood; and that was not part of his plans. Weddings were talked of, after all Tim was now 22 years old and still remained single. It seemed as if expectations were on everyone's minds.

Tim felt the peer pressure; "Time you settled down and started a family, young man," was the frequent comment.

Tim's life was changing, he knew it, and that it happened the way it did amazingly became a part of the basis for this book as you read it now. As Tim sees life, now, he realises it could have all been so different, as is it with so many others who were not brave enough. Tim is thankful for the love and companionship shared over many years. No regrets, no messy situations to ask forgiveness for; just a wonderful life, as it was meant to be.

## Society Expectations – Family Pressure – All Getting Too Much

For some reason, not known to himself, Tim was feeling quite frightened at all that was going on around him, even wedding plans and the like; for he found himself caught up in the whirlwind of "doing the right thing," just as his older brothers (and, come to think about it, all his nephews and the lads he went to school with) had done: following societal expectations of finding a girlfriend, courting, getting married, having a family, and living happily ever after. The right thing in the eyes of the family, perhaps, but what about Tim's feelings, his deep desires?

It was something that was beyond Tim's control and definitely not what Tim wanted, or had even contemplated. As the days, weeks, & months passed, and the date of the wedding was being discussed, Tim was preoccupied with coming to terms with his inner self. What was he to do?! Continue with society's expectations and what everyone wanted (and was planning), which would force Tim into a future that was at odds with what he felt, and what he deep down knew he wanted. With the level of fear growing inside Tim, he decided it had to end and planned to do just that … but at this point, he was not sure how to achieve this.

## First "Cottage" Experience

A few hundred yards from his girlfriend's house was a public convenience (toilet) on the roadside, opened for all to use, and one night Tim needed to relieve himself and went in on his way home. Tim was surprised to see a guy in there whom he knew to be his auntie's neighbour, who we knew as Gordon. He was single and in his late 30s, and lived alone. Tim ignored him at first, but then acknowledged his hello. Gordon moved next to Tim with his huge erect penises in his hand, beckoning to Tim to touch it.

Tim froze for second; whilst he felt pleasure in seeing Gordon's erect penis, what would happen if someone came in? Even worse if it was someone Tim knew, or even the local bobby. Tim panicked, his heart starting to beat very fast; his body shaking, Tim quickly fastened his trousers, left, and made for home.

Tim saw Gordon a few times after that, and often in the same toilet, where Gordon would be masturbating himself for Tim to see. All this happened so quickly, and Tim felt himself drawn to see if Gordon was in there each time Tim went home past the same public toilet.

Although no closeness between them took place Tim had become aware of an awakening within him. He was now 23 years of age and genuinely knew nothing like this had ever crossed his mind.

## Coming to Terms With One's Inner Thoughts

Tim, having come to peace with his inner mind, reached the conclusion it was necessary to end the relationship with his fiancé. A silly quarrel one evening gave Tim the chance to carry out his plan; he decided it was time not to see his girlfriend again, and they never contacted each other from that day on.

Her mother caused many problems, and even sought out his mother in the hairdresser's, to give her opinions, so to speak, though Tim's mum never divulged what was said. However, Tim knew he had made the right decision, having asked for the ring back, and they never saw each other again. Tim heard she married and had eight children. Tim remembered thinking to himself, *ending the engagement was a lucky escape!*

Following the cancellation of the engagement to his fiancé, and consequent separation, Tim lived at home with his parents and younger sister, enjoying a simple, uncomplicated life – helping with the decorating and relieving his mother of many household chores which Tim enjoyed doing.

That summer, Tim's mother went on holiday with his sister and her family for a week and Tim was left to look after his dad.

# Life Changing Decision and Experiencing One's First "Love"

Tim had made up his mind that evening to go to the cinema in town, and so he got ready to do so. In those days, even a simple outing like this meant a suit with a smart collar and tie. Arriving at the cinema of his choice, he noticed a guy outside, also smartly dressed. Tim didn't buy his ticket straight away, but waited a while. It seemed the other guy was doing exactly the same and trying to attract Tim's attention. Beginning to feel nervous, Tim started to walk towards the tram, and home, when he noticed the stranger was during the same. What was Tim going to do? Thinking quickly and looking across the road, Tim saw another tram going in a different direction but still towards home.

Tim got on and so did the other guy. A short distance along the line, and Tim continuing to feel nervous if not afraid, Tim got off the tram, followed by the other guy. Tim, thinking it would put him off, went across the road to the Orient Cinema, only to be followed, again, by the same guy. Having separately bought a ticket, they ended up sitting in the same row but not next to one another. One has to remember, unlike today, these were very difficult times. It certainly was not the done thing for two strange men to be seen sitting next to each other, or even two male friends sitting near to each other, come to think of it.

Tim knew he had done nothing wrong, but it seemed he was having new experiences all the time, and it was frightening figuring out how to shake the guy off.

Once the film had finished, and returning to the city on the same train, they sat together. Although on one hand being petrified, Tim also, in a strange way, felt happy they were sitting next to each other. They talked and very quickly realised they were both petrified. By this time Peter had introduced himself and they talked until Peter, who lived in Kidderminster, had to get of the tram to catch his last bus at 2200 hours. They agreed to meet again same place, same time the following week.

## An Evening's Reflection and What Might Follow

Continuing the remainder of his journey home, Tim reflected upon the evening and his first experience of what would transpire to be the start of Tim's first gay relationship. Tim felt a sense of relief, inside, but was very troubled as to what was happening.

The next time Tim & Peter met they discussed going on a short holiday to Llandudno. Oh, this in itself was an experience for Tim; holidays were only for the wealthy at that time.

Peter asked Tim to make the arrangements, as it would be difficult for him to explain to his parents why he was going on holiday with a mate, but it was more convenient for Tim, as a neighbour had relatives who owned a guest house.

## First Weekend Away With Another … Man!

Together they went to Llandudno for a short trip and shared a bed, a first for Tim in any circumstances. Peter was just as Tim imagined he would be. Peter was kind, he was gentle, and like any true friends they enjoyed the time together, doing the usual holiday things but with extreme caution, as required.

Peter gave Tim a beautiful introduction to gay sex. They shared the moment with ecstasy and upon investigation Tim realised Peter only had one testicle. At first this bothered Tim, but he was reassured that this was due to a boyhood accident.

This brief trip away, and Tim's first experience of sharing a bed with another man and the pleasurable activity that took place, was to be a one off for them both. For although they spoke every day for the next six months that followed, there wasn't to be another opportunity as they both lived at home and it was definitely not "the done thing" to invite another man to one's bedroom when living under the same roof as one's parents.

## Wrong Side of the Law – As It Was Until 1967

Peter was caught up in a police raid, which wasn't unusual in those times, and Tim could only contact him through the understanding neighbour who allowed them the use of her phone, for in the 1960s the majority of homes did not have the luxury of a landline and mobile phones were not even invented.

## Being In Love For The First Time – Comes To an End

As time passed their love waned, but they didn't fall out and Peter reappears later in this story.

Tim carried on with his life. At the time Tim knew little or nothing about the new life/pathway he had found and could only believe that others like himself were destined for a lonely and fearsome life.

Tim did know, however, if someone male looked at him in a certain way how one was meant to react. He was frightened … Although, unbeknownst to Tim, having little experience with what in gay terminology is called "GAYDAR", this look given & received did not communicate anger, or suggest physical violence. This was a strange predicament; such experiences were all new to Tim and to a certain extent caused confusion. Little by little he was becoming aware of the serious situations occurring around him, especially after the one person he had met and fallen in love with had said it was better not to maintain contact.

## Cruising Escapades – No Other Option

Tim's grandmother was alive; she was blind and living with Tim's aunt, his father's sister, and he occasionally visited her. This was one escape Tim had from living at home with his parents.

Tim had done just that one Tuesday evening in the summer, and left to return home by bus. Tim knew that by changing his route he would have the opportunity to pass a public convenience/ toilet that was on the way home. Tim's auntie lived in an older area where several houses shared a toilet, and he didn't fancy that.

As Tim entered the public convenience, a guy he saw most days on the bus to work came in through another entrance and stood near Tim and smiled.

They smiled at each other and then the guy showed Tim what Tim hoped he would: his erect penis. Tim, once again, was nervous, his heart pounding away, feeling very afraid, and so he made his way out and began crossing the road but then decided he would walk the remaining distance home.

Of course, Tim was being followed and eventually the guy was walking side by side. Tim was panicking. *What does this guy want? Is he going to attack me?* Tim heard the guy speak to him but pretended not to. Tim also heard, the next time, when the chap repeated, "Did you like what you saw?" Tim, being too nervous to speak, blubbered an answer and then heard, "Have you any-where to go?" Tim replied he didn't and was on his way home after visiting his grandmother.

It didn't deter this guy, who by now had told him his name was Do. They discussed where each other worked and the coincidence of seeing each other daily. Tim discovered he worked in a shoe shop and caught that particular bus to get Tim to work for a nine o'clock start. Do told him where he lived, a road where they had to pass to Tim's home, but when they got to that point and it was parting time, he asked if they could walk further together. Do was nicely spoken, dressed as Tim would have wished, and said he was of Irish descent and had several brothers and sisters.

## Travelling Home – a Diversion On The Way

As they approached a pub near to where they both caught the bus, Do, who now asked Tim to call him Don, suggested they went in for a drink. Tim didn't know what to say, he'd never been inside a pub before, but he agreed.

As they entered the pub, the door to the gents was right there to the left. Don turned to go in and Tim followed, wondering what on earth was happening. But he needn't have worried. As they both washed their hands, Don turned and asked, "May I kiss you?" … nothing else. Tenderly they embraced, and that was to be expected because, as they continued to speak to each other as they walked towards the pub, "I think I've fallen in love with you," Don said.

By now, as they were finishing their drinks, Tim felt so relieved. He was pleased everything was going well and he didn't feel quite so afraid.

Don insisting walking Tim's home, despite protests. Tim thought this was the way that things happen, and he was happy with it, for it felt as if they were together, so to speak.

## How Will Mum React – As Mums Always Do?

Tim had only one small shandy but already felt dizzy and couldn't help wondering – it was a cool summer evening, his mother might be taking the air outside his home as she often did. As they turned the corner to approach Tim's house, his fears were fulfilled. Tim's mum was there. Tim paused, how was he going to explain why Don was with him? However, there was no going back … to do so would have said more than needed to be said.

Hellos and introductions over, Tim felt much calmer, and why shouldn't he? After all, Tim was simply introducing a friend to Mum.

Tim's mum said to Don, "You're the young man who sells me my shoes at Playfair." Don acknowledged she was correct. "Are you coming in for a cup of tea?" she asked. There was no awkwardness; why should there be? Mums know, and she'd been through all this with the other six children. There was no need for Tim to have been afraid.

As Don got up to go, after drinking his tea, Tim's mum said, so easily, "See Don to the door, then." If she noticed that Tim took a little longer than might have been expected, she didn't comment.

Of course, there was much to talk about, and in the strangeness of the situation Tim felt he had found the beginning of a new life. If this was being in love, Tim relished every moment.


## Meeting Up Each Week – But Needed To Be Discreet

Tim and Don had declared their feelings for each other and, albeit with some difficulty because of their home commitments, had managed to fulfil their love at a hotel they never visited most Wednesday evenings for dinner. Neither drove a car, so staying the night was convenient. Tim and Don had agreed, because of the times they were living in, when homosexuality was frowned upon, to say the least – not to mention being illegal. They had, like all men in their situation, to be careful, and so agreed not to be on the same bus every day in order to maintain their discreetness.


## Hobbies and Female Friends

Their discussions about life, the future, hobbies, etc. revealed that they were both involved in ballroom dancing. Tim had ended his career prior to meeting Don, who was still active on that scene with his partner Joan – a dance partner only – and danced at the

Tower Ballroom in Blackpool, which they both knew well. Joan accepted to a point that he wasn't at all interested in her physically, but never gave up completely. She was always around, so to speak, and would make arrangements knowing she was interfering, but they had danced together for many years, so she couldn't be cast out of his life and Tim understood that.

## Experiencing Open Relationship – But Only One-sided

Don's family totally accepted he was the way he was and were happy to see Don and Tim together. Don would occasionally fail to keep promises, to meet, without telling Tim of his intentions, which made Tim query the situation. Don never gave reasons, but Joan was more than happy to reveal Don had been seeing his previous partner, Michael. Don and Michael had split up some months before Don met Tim.

## Two's Company But Three's a Crowd

Loving Don as he did, Tim kept silent and they continued to meet each other. As Tim and Don progressed their relationship it was the old "three in this relationship" scenario, and as much as she was told not to, Joan turned up everywhere except for Wednesday evenings, which she learned were taboo. It was as if Joan thought she belonged in the family, but as time went on, they proved their love for Tim.

On one occasion Joan questioned Tim on his knowledge of queers, the gay world, homosexuality and what they got their kicks out of. Tim was very careful with his answers, not only because with his brief experience he truly didn't know many of the answers. Tim's gay lifestyle remained in its infancy and he was very innocent on the subject.

Anyway, on one occasion thereafter, when the guys had arranged to meet on a Sunday afternoon, Don failed to appear, so Tim took himself off to the cinema alone to see a film called "An Affair to Remember".

When Tim and Don met in the evening, Tim told him about his trip to the cinema and the film he had seen. Don asked to be told all about the film that Tim enjoyed so much, and on hearing all about it, Don said "Would you like to see it again?"

"I would love to," was Tim's reply, to which Don replied he'd also like to see it. Without hesitation they got on the bus and were back at the next showing of the film. Don told everyone what happened and relived the moment for some time afterwards!

## Female Support – Or Was It a Sign of Jealousy?

Joan wasn't happy; she said that in all their years together, she and Don had never been to the cinema and remarked it must be love, and that it spoke volumes that they were happy despite Don's wanderings. Don and Tim's affair continued, with both of them remaining at home with their respective parents.

## One Family Acceptance But Discord at Home

Tim was content and well accepted by Don's family. Tim was included in all the gatherings, and being Irish, there were many! Tim's mum, in turn, liked Don enough to call him Tim's partner, although that was not the done thing in the sixties/seventies.

For many reasons, Tim's life at home was becoming problematic, and he decided to move out. When Tim disclosed this to his brother nearest to him in age, Tim was told he could move in with them whenever he wanted to do so.

Tim had done just that and continued to see Don until …

## An Expected Encounter

Don had failed to turn up on this particular Saturday evening, so Tim decided to go home to his brother's. When Tim arrived, there was a strange car on the drive, but he went in all the same and found a stranger there watching TV with Tim's brother.

Tim's brother was surprised to see Tim so early, and introduced Eric, a friend from work. Tim's brother said, "Eric wanted to see this film, but Eric's mother didn't want it on, so we said Eric could come here."

Who was Tim to disagree? The guy seemed friendly enough and as the evening progressed became concerned that Tim wasn't in a good place to see the film. Tim wasn't interested in the film anyway, but it came to the point where Eric offered to give up his seat on the sofa to Tim, and Eric would sit on the floor. Tim wouldn't hear of it and said he would sit on the floor. That agreed, Tim was sitting in front of Eric, and little by little Eric was opening his knees and pulling closer to Tim until Tim was aware he could feel Eric's arousal on the back of his neck.

## Sharing a Bed With a Total Stranger – What Could Happen?

The film ended, discussions took place, and a cuppa was served. It was now bedtime, and then came the shock …

Tim's brother said, quite casually, "We've said Eric can stay here, save him traveling in the dark, is that alright with you? You will both manage, it's a double bed!"

Settling into bed, Tim soon became aware that Eric had ideas of his own. He soon showed he was very capable of going through with what he had planned; Eric was not a novice and helped Tim climax through the ecstasy and joy, making sure there was no evidence left to be found. They didn't sleep a great deal, content with the closeness of each other's bodies.

By the time they awoke in the morning, Tim's brother and sister-in-law had gone off to work. The two of them just lay there in bed, talking of Tim moving into Eric's home.

Eric had recently parted from a long-term relationship and his mother had indicated that in the event of Eric meeting someone new, she would be happy for him.

Eric was concerned Tim was in the wrong environment, after he made him aware that his brother had recently lost the tenancy of a pub; therefore, being effectively homeless, the council had allocated them the house where Tim's brother and his wife were now staying. It was a very rough area. Tim was likewise very concerned for his brother & sister-in-law.

## One Night Sharing a Bed With a "Stranger" – and Life Changes

Tim and Eric went off to see Eric's mother, and Tim moved in. Very surprisingly for Tim, even Eric's dad approved, and was happy he had someone to "share the gardening," as he put it.

Tim and Eric were together for eight years, which were basically good for them, but his mother was very demanding and the culmination was that they were determined to move into a place of their own.

Tim's brother, Noah, had a colleague who was in property and let Tim & Eric have a new-build apartment in a very nice area on the outskirts of town. They were good together in every way; physically, sexually, and emotionally, being relaxed with each other after six years of living with a dominant mother who insisted on being part of their lives and constantly inviting the neighbour's daughter, who had grown up with Eric, for breakfast, dinner, and tea, and as the daughter thought she stood a chance with Eric, she never refused.

## Living Together – The Challenges, The Dangers

Although Tim and Eric were happy enough together, they got into financial difficulties, mainly because Eric had been used to having everything he wanted with his mum at his side. It proved difficult without this support.

Their flat was beautifully furnished, but Eric had seen a very smart radiogram (as it was called all those years ago). In fact, it was in a shop quite close to where Eric worked, and he knew the salesman, who had agreed to let them have it on the right terms.

This scenario was at odds with Tim, for he had been brought up with the mantra "if you can't afford it … save for it." It bothered him greatly, for living beyond one's means was seriously frowned upon in those days (and it was not until well into the 80s that owning a credit card started to become popular).

Purchasing the "radiogram" on credit created even more financial problems, and they agreed to part, with Eric moving back to his mum's. Of course, Eric met someone new. Tim remained living in their flat.

## It's Not Always What It First Appears – But First impressions Can Be Devastating

Several weeks after Eric moved out of their flat and went back to live with his Mum, one of Tim's colleagues, Neil, invited Tim out for dinner and a drink and inevitably stayed the night. There was no intention of anything happening, for Neil and his partner had been good friends to Tim during his problems, and in any case, no one knew that Tim had had a small operation on his coccyx and was in no condition for sex. The only people that knew were the couple in the flat below, who were helping Tim in and out of the bath (she, being a nursing sister, was kind to Tim, so that was the situation).

Although Eric had returned to live with his mum, he continued to have a key to their flat to enable Eric to let himself in whenever, however required.

Neil was finishing his breakfast, comprising of tea & toast, when Eric let himself in, and the accusations flew; after which Eric made his way to tell Tim's mother what he had seen, or *thought* he had seen. She was very angry. Tim was left with a great deal of debt, which controlled his life for a long time after that.

Sadly, for Tim this was the last straw, and totally destroyed what was once such a beautiful and meaningful relationship with Eric.


## If Only! But Young and Naïve


It was sometime later, when Tim was in town shopping during his lunch break, that he bumped into Joan, who you may recall was the "third person" in Tim's relationship with Don. Joan was pleased to see Tim and asked about his life. Tim assured her he was good and had a partner of some years. Joan's reply took Tim back, as she declared that's what Don was planning. Don was worried that Tim was so new to "the scene" and that's why Don got Joan to ask Tim all those questions as she did.

When Joan previously asked Tim if he knew what "cottaging" was or meant Tim said yes, having a holiday in a cottage; and when Tim was asked if he know what camp meant, he gave a similarly simple answer. Joan explained, "Don loved your answers displaying so much naïveté and was looking for a house to buy so that he could ask you to move in with him and break with Michael for good, for Don loved you so much and so did the family." Tim and Joan, after finishing their conversation, went their separate ways, Tim reflecting on Joan's comments, thinking if only … not so young and naïve, things with Don may have turned out different … "Hey-ho," that's what growing up is all about: learning life's lessons and focusing looking forward, not backwards.

## Another "Closure" From Past Relationships – Another Life Lesson

Tim, several months later, met Donal's mother (as Tim found out later to be Don's correct name). She held Tim tenderly, just as if Tim was her lost son.

When Tim spoke of Donal, his mum said, "He loved you so much. Donal and John moved to Weston-super-Mare and died there six months later of gout at the age of 33." Tim & Donal's Mum shared tears of joy and thankfulness that, between them, they had known this guy, though sometimes unreliable and not always showing up when arranged to do so. God bless him, Tim knew Donal had taught him so much on this rocky road.

Perhaps the inquirers to this subject will at some stage come to realise the intensity of the love between two men or two women has the same depth as that between heterosexuals. It can, and does, extend to families as a whole. To be accepted by each other's families is a wonderful thing. Breakups, which are inevitable, do happen. The sadness Tim had was shared by all, and as in this case, the passing of one's partner can, and does, affect so many people.

## Life's Basic Requirements – It's Human Nature – Is It Not?

If you are reading this book as a gay person you will be aware of the story, I'm sure, but if you are standing on the edge, so to speak, you may be thinking the life of any one of us consists of a constant search for sexual activity and the like. ... Well, let me put you straight right away: just as heterosexuals do, the majority of us are simply, firstly and foremostly, searching for a partner, a partner we can share our life with.

# "What Is Meant By The Word Partner?" Do I Hear You Ask?

A partner is a person we can share our lives with, all the good and not so good moments, go to sleep next and wake up next to, build a future with; someone who cares for us on a mutual basis. Someone who gives and receives love, someone to explore inner life's experiences with. To have respect for each other, a desire to be an integral part of each other's life as one traverses along life's rollercoaster ride. Of course, there has to be love and trust, and that in itself is the basis of sharing a sexual relationship – but *trust* is the overarching ingredient to create and maintain, any successful relationship, whether it be heterosexual or gay … true?

Yes, naturally we're looking not only at the outward appearance but what the general character of the person shows us. Physique, outward strength, of course. So, what is different about us? We look, we wander beyond the clothed figure that we see. We all, every one of us, want to be satisfied in a sexual way; it's the way we're made. Whenever someone realises you're a couple their mind strays to the bedroom activities, wondering who is doing what to whom, and their imagination runs away with them.

As gays we have to work, eat, cook, clean, and all the other mundane things; to top it all off, we don't have time to worry about you, as long as you're looking after each other and others around you.

Yes, we too, have made mistakes in our choices, but that's life, isn't it ?!

The old saying is "size doesn't matter, it's the tenderness that counts." We all know how true that is.

Question: does the above not also apply to heterosexual partners? … So is there any difference?

The one thing that needs to be remembered is that homosexuality is nothing new; it doesn't originate from any specific era. The dictionary states the fact: one person attracted to another of the same sex. How difficult is that? And what is there to dispute?

When you think of Jesus, all those hundreds of years ago, disciples working around and for him, groups of young men. How sure can we be there was no attraction between them? There hasn't been a change of pattern as to the designs of our bodies, male or female. We are all made in God and, we are told, some a little, or in some cases a lot different to one another.

For all these hundreds of years the "sin" (A sin? Or just seeking love?) has been around the world; it wasn't the act of intercourse that was the problem, it was man's meaning of the word and the interpretation.

Surely over these years they that have truly experienced love, and I mean love, from a heartfelt kiss to full penetration, are those qualified to give opinions? They who are sadly deprived have no stance in the discussions, being rejected is no excuse. People are and always have been such bigots on the subject. To have felt the warmth of love, to experience, and what's more, to have known and held another's sexual organs at the height of togetherness in love and then be broken apart must have been a terrible price to pay, but God knows it happened for many years, and for what reason? Simply to stop, or attempt to stop, good decent men from loving each other. Believe it or not, the years that many of us alive today lived through in fear were simply because we saw the greatest gift of God … love!

Like all, or most, things in life, along came a government willing to make changes; and doesn't it reflect the situation that among their own number were, as in all walks of life, men who were different. Perhaps it wasn't before time and so much damage had been done, not to mention the loss of lives.

## A Well-Intended Word From Dad

Although his dad had not really discussed Tim's sexuality, he did one day say to Tim:

"However you live your life is up to you — be careful, and don't get into trouble. There are some pubs in town you don't want to go into … "

He went on to mention the names of the two places Tim would know. Tim acknowledged the conversation, he had to.

## Remembering Dad's well intended words ... but Tim's inner voice says different

Tim's friends frequented the places mentioned, but Tim himself had only looked in one, which was situated down some stairs. Tim had found it uncomfortable and saw his dad's point. However, "Jimmy's bar" was more familiar to all, at the bottom of New Street, its proper name being St James Bar. This bar is probably still there, under the demolished buildings; what stories those ruins could tell!

The other one that Tim's dad had mentioned was through some iron gates and visibly tiled in ornate green tiles; it was called the Exchange Bar. Tim's fears, like those of many, were of being trapped in there in a raid. Today a pedestrian slope around the corner from Jimmy's bar hides the mystery of the past.

Where Tim's friends met, and *the* pub to meet in, was the Trocadero in Temple Street. All life there was sectioned off into areas where groups of all kinds of gays would congregate.

Everyone knew it was where *"those people"* met, but basically the clientele was ordinary everyday guys, all likeminded, either meeting friends or in the hope of picking someone up to take back to their flat for sex. It wasn't a secret; they came alone, had a chat, and left together. It was also a place where the occasional celebrity, "Lord so and so" and the like came for a change from the press and prying eyes, to be themselves for a while with likeminded people.

# Just Good Friends – Sadly?
## And Societal Expectations and Compliance

Although many of Tim's close friends were around the same age as himself, as Tim sat now, he was aware of so many who had passed away through everyday illnesses. Still, his memories were good.

There used to be parties to go to, the ones that the select few would be invited to, and the ones where those who got word would go. Tim stayed in the group he knew and looked after him. Without a doubt, he was aware there were a certain few who wanted to share Tim's life more closely. Just a dance or two, a close embrace and yes, the inevitable fumble, but Tim always knew he had a lift home in safety without getting involved.

Times change and so do people, and from Tim's ballroom dancing days he often saw his instructor, David, around town. David had his own reputation – simply "*fabulous!*"

David was one of two guys Tim knew who, if you did, "*you had made it*" – that seemed to be the expression used. Tim would be walking around somewhere in the city and that prestigious blue Austin A40 would draw up alongside Tim, but he always resisted. Away went the car to the sounds of *"you will one day"* and Tim did, but as they say, disappointment follows fame – David wasn't *the* David Tim thought he'd be … is enough to say here. Tim wasn't into David's' "ways," so to speak.


## Life Back Home With Mum and Dad and a New Adventure

Tim was very happy, as he was now living back home with his parents. His life was restricted but had managed to put behind him some of the problems; not of his own making. but he had lived in places he'd rather not have been, with an Auntie who did "her own thing" and waited up for Tim on the nights she was there. Sometimes it would be one, two or three in the morning. Tim had just stayed away walking the streets alone, crying, wondering why he was in this situation … dreaming of his own home and wondering where Mr Right was, and when would appear, and put everything right. A warm cosy bed with fresh linen, an arm that was attached to a warm friendly body, shower fresh, and who knows after that … ?

Sex wasn't the be all and end all for Tim. He knew things could have been easier if he thought differently, but Tim could wait.

Tim's friends understood his point, but still when opportunities were offered, they'd encourage him to take them. He didn't want to.

## Financial Constraints Continue – True …
## Yes, Genuinely True Friends

Going back to when Tim had problems, financially, the few friends he had around him at that time did rally round him genuinely and sincerely. They didn't, and he wouldn't have wanted them to, offer financial help and support. Tim was where he was and had hoped to change things around him. Tim held his head up high; his friends always invited him to share their lives, and he did something he hadn't done before: Tim walked into pubs to meet them and, although desperately embarrassed, never had to buy a round. They knew Tim wasn't in a position to do that and cleverly covered the situation. He was so grateful he could make half a bitter or a bitter lemon last for as long as he had to; that was his wish, they knew he wasn't a drinker. it was a respite and he loved dressing up with somewhere to go. There were always people to meet with, someone to go for a natter, and often refused. That may sound arrogant, but it wasn't meant to be – he had a reputation and it didn't get any easier.

## Maintaining High Standards – Especially Appearance.

Tim had always been used to looking well presented. His parents had a friend who was a tailor and from his early teens had made Tim's suits – that's what they wore in those days, a well-tailored suit and crisp shirt. Some like Tim had a loose collar starched so stiffly, if someone called you and you turned around quickly there was risk of an injury. Tim remembered the competition between himself and the guy in the crowd (Gary) over cufflinks.

Gary worked on ships between the UK and America. He got home quite frequently and joined his friends when he could. Gary was a little loud at times, talking mainly about the money he earned and the origin of his clothes, oh, and yes, about his cuff links. He joked with Tim about this and was always prepared to discuss the subject. But whilst Gary said his always come from some state stall on one of his trips, Tim had his own supplier nearer to home: the lady on the market stall who sold the most fabulous earrings, which were fashionable in those days. She would wait for Tim to come on Saturdays, showing him her latest purchases and saying, "These are gorgeous." Sometimes beautiful stone, sometimes sparkly, even on the odd occasion the imitation mink. She knew Tim could transform them into cufflinks like no one else had seen or were likely to.

In Tim's own way he was a quiet chap, some said, well-spoken and of course presented himself well. For all this Tim knew you had earnt that snob reputation, but he knew he wasn't; he was generally afraid of life itself. For most, the standard dress code, growing up in the early 60s, reflected whether one was going to the office, going to a restaurant, going to the cinema, or simply going out for an evening with friends, looking smart … wearing a shirt, collar and tie was the norm (and Tim expected it).

Reflecting on the niceness of being well presented, Tim recalled the lovely brown Prince of Wales check suit he had made, a change to the inevitable charcoal grey. It was teamed with the usual white shirt, canary yellow tie, and as was the mood, yellow socks. The item of the day was what were known as ginger suede shoes.

## Never Too Old for Well-Meant Motherly Advice

Tim was ready to meet his friends. His mum was talking to neighbours outside the front door, as they did in those days, as Tim left the house with a cheery "See you later."

He wasn't far down the road when he heard his mother call, upon which he turned around to go and find out what she wanted. As she approached Tim, she said, "Do you feel good?"

"Yes," Tim replied, feeling like their cats whiskers.

"I mean this," she said, "if you could see yourself from behind, in those shoes, you wouldn't. Walk properly, walk like a man." All this to a man in his late 20s, on the receiving end of a well meant telling off from Mum. From that moment Tim has never minced again, and hopes he never will.

## The Peacemaker – With Unexpected Consequences

You may recall, Tim mentioned his early years and his older brother. As the time passed by, life being what it is, they didn't see a great deal of each other, and his brother being married, he didn't visit the family home very often.

Tim could remember the days when his brother was courting his now wife. They always seemed to be falling out, and that's really where Tim became useful, for when this happened his brother would ask Tim to take notes to her, apologies, forgiveness, who knows, as they eventually married, but he felt he had helped in some small way.

Whenever he had to go there her brother was always around; a tall good-looking guy, he was in the Air Force and always seemed to be combing his hair in the mirror, and would catch Tim's eye. He was nice, but so what … For at the time Tim was totally oblivious to know what the future would hold.

As the years went by they had no contact, but whenever the sister-in-law visited there was always a lot of conversation surrounding her brother, Bernard, or "Bunny", as he was known.

Bunny had this "friend", very wealthy, a big house, nice area and so on … Tim could not fathom out why they had this big posh house where they lived, but, hey-ho, life seemed strange to Tim then, being so innocent of such matters.


## A Few Years Later – All Revealed

Then one day, years later of course, Tim was working in a shoe shop when the manager from another branch called to say he had no staff and help was needed. Tim's manager immediately asked if Tim would go. It wasn't far from where he and Eric used to live, so yes, he happily said he'd go.

Dressed as a good salesman was in those days, he arrived at the shop. The guy there introduced himself as David; he was nice and friendly and spoke a lot about living in the flat above the shop of his friend, Bunny – Tim paused for a few seconds and thought, *Bunny! … No … it couldn't be …* But it was! It was hugs and kisses between the brothers in law.


## Reunited and Now The Four Boys – Life Long Friendship

There were, as in all families, weddings, funerals, and get togethers, and mostly all the four boys would be there together, but beyond such events, Bunny and David were always part of Tim's life. They would see each other every week or on a regular basis. They were always friends but also had their own circle of friends. It was a friendship that lasted many years until they both, Bunny and David, passed away in recent years.

## Brotherly Acceptance? – Society Dictates

Tim's elder brother thought the world of them both; he talked to them, he praised Bunny (remember … his brother-in-law) for achieving the standard of life they did and said they were fine examples of good citizens.

"*But* Bunny and David *were homosexual,*" you will say … and you are correct! And they loved each other, man to man, a friendship Tim's brother accepted … but he didn't (or could not) come to terms with the extending that acceptance to his own brother, Tim, and his partner … strange, isn't it? Tim never received such a much-needed compliment from his own brother, but remember, Tim was still "a queer" in his brother eyes, and sadly, that's mankind, however close you may be.

## Living Back Home With Mum and Dad – Some Escape and Recreation Needed

A couple of hours at the gym was his recreation, spending his evenings/weekends there. The guys were friendly enough and when they called Tim "Pretty boy" and started to adjust their "kit" when they sat opposite him, Tim smiled and wondered where their wedding rings had gone?!

However, there was one guy (whose name, Tim later discovered, was Chris) who always noticed Tim was sitting alone and, on one occasion, asked Tim to share his pot of tea. They did. After a short while the curtains around them closed and the fumbling began ... there was only fumbling, but they were both naked, and anyway, was this the right place, with others nearby aware of what was happening?

For Tim it was a moment he'd waited for for so long. Having both climaxed, with great excitement and feeling of satisfaction, they wiped each other clean and were making plans to meet again.

They exchanged phone numbers etc. (there hadn't been much time to do so in the time before, and anyway, there were bigger things in hand! ... And to talk about).

Meet again? They certainly did, and as weeks of sharing time together quickly extended into several months, Tim and Chris discussed taking their relationship further.


## A New Partner and New Home – But Was It Two-way?

It wasn't long before a house had been purchased and they moved in together. Life was good; they were comfortable, families supported them, driving lessons were achieved and then a new car purchased. Tim took his test and passed also before purchasing his own car.

But there was more to life than this material existence. Chris had worked in a hospital for many years and always preferred night shifts. It didn't seem a problem at first. The bond created between Tim and Chris, apart from being a new experience for Tim, created the excitement of being able to look forward to spending a romantic and fulfilling two days together during Chris' off days each week ... but for how long?

## A Surprising Visitor From the Past!

Tim was now working in the local florist. Late one afternoon there was a surprise visitor. In earlier pages it was said Peter, Tim's first love would return, and he did … Yes, looking up to see who had walked into the florist, Tim saw Peter standing there.

Peter was visiting the area on business and decided to say hi to Tim before catching the train back home. Not to take up where they left off, but to tell Tim he was having medical help for the state of his mind.

Tim recalls that Peter was a good Christian man. Peter had met a guy, they had had sex, several times apparently, and loved each other … and then Peter went to church. Yes! You're right, the vicar was Peter's new love.

Peter and the Vicar hadn't discussed careers, little non-entities like that; they found joy with each other as they knew best – love and sex, like so many others.

Sadly, the situation made Peter ill for whatever reason. Peter couldn't get over it, it played on his mind. To the majority it would have been another sexual escapade, but this was not the case.

It wasn't the man, the clergyman, it wasn't the fact that Peter was a well-known businessman. It was, as he told Tim, a bond between two people, two men, that was crime in the eyes of others.


## Being Gay – The Punishment Willingly Dispensed … And by "Medical Professionals"

Like so many others, Peter explained to Tim, he was subjected to the vilest of treatments. Shut away in rooms that no human would subject animals to, and what is worse, taken to and left in rooms with a screen showing naked men abusing themselves to all disgusting lengths, and for what reason? To cure him … of what? The Sin of falling in love with another man.

Tim was feeling very sad, shaking his head, as he thinks of the courage of his dear friend.

It was now time for Tim to close the shop for the day and there was much for Tim and Peter to catch up on. Tim invited Peter to join him on the journey back home and to meet Chris, Tim's partner at the time.

Not long after Tim and Peter arrived home, it was time for Chris to leave for work and commence his customary night shift, leaving Tim and Peter to continue talking.

The next few hours passed quickly, and it very soon became time for Peter to leave in order to take the last train home.

## Being Gay – Society's Reaction – "It's a Disease – and Can Be Treated"

Tim was extremely troubled to learn what had happened to Peter and Peter's mental health, to such an extent that for several months thereafter Tim made the regular journey (with Chris' consent) to visit Peter. On occasions, when Tim visited, he would find his friend in the craziest times of distress, having been continually being subjected to attempts to cure (change) him.

Like so much of history, little is known about the genuine facts and the endless number of other gay men who were also shut away in those inhumane buildings, officially called sanitoriums. Peter never said what he was being subjected to, or about his abusers, for that is certainly what they were.

Peter is remembered as a very handsome man, dark with black hair. Always immaculate in his dress and courteous in his manner. Loving to his parents and brother.

For that which seems to be the traits of any gay man capable of giving and sharing love with his fellow human beings, he suffered at the hands of bullies doing so on behalf and instructed by bullies.

When Peter wrote a letter and asked for Tim and Chris to visit him in hospital, they never could have imagined what they would or might find: a cripple of a man, s fraction of his size, afraid and weeping at the very thought of a knock on his cell door, leaving a memory so sick one almost wants to refrain from writing about it. Today in a modern, free for all world, where privilege is misconstrued and man considers himself as having mental health issues, this practice continues to escape notice.

## Being Gay – Society Persecution – The Pain Becomes Too Much

Peter's life ended one Sunday evening, after Tim and Chris had been alerted that Peter was missing, having been discharged, not cured or changed, from hospital. He had been with his uncle, who would arrive to comfort and consult him

Tim and Chris visited any possible place Peter may have gone to before finding him, sadly too late, at his place of work. At the top of the staircase, in the building Peter had worked so hard to achieve, they found him very tragically killed by the very tool that earned him his living … gas. Peter had taken the gas which he used to give comfort to so many, for Peter was a dental surgeon.

## Being Gay – The Heartbreak … Was It Fair? … Was It Humane?

If, like the writer, you have tears streaming down your face just reading this, remember this is only one case in hundreds. Tim continuing, at this point in time, to be living with Chris, they both attended the funeral, for as Peter's parents had said, "You were his escape," although his dad did not accept him being as he was, queer. Peter died shortly after, his thoughts unknown.

Such heartbreak arises from such situations in life, and such grief stays with us forever. So few of another generation read of

such events; so many never know they happened, happily putting themselves into moments of temptation for the experience.
Simply bragging of the number of one's conquests is all too easy
and is common place in a world, always has been, and always will.

Each story in a newspaper has a new or old view on homosexuality, whichever is appropriate, of that gay world, as it was
so often called. They were times when there were differences
between what we called dandies and a homosexual world, but
they were discreet in their behaviour.

Death certainly was the punishment of the time.

## Gay Relationships Versus Religion

Whilst writing, life goes on around us, as we would expect. It is
worthy of note, especially at this point, that in today's newspaper
the headline reads: "Catholic Church will not sanction gay unions." So be it. Having written the last few pages, one wonders
if the hearts of the powers who make such decisions could not be
moved. In case you are not aware, let us look at those headlines.
"The Vatican has decreed that the Catholic Church cannot bless
same-sex unions because God cannot bless sin. The Vatican's or-
thodoxy office … " the congregation for the doctrine of faith,
issued a formal response to a question about whether Catholic
clergy can bless gay unions. The answer, contained in a two-page
explanation published in seven languages and approved by Pope
Francis, was negative. The obvious question that follows being:
how many more dental surgeons, clergymen, etc.?

## Not Being True to One's Self, Nor One's Spouse ...
## Just Because of Society's Expectations

Tim remembered two good friends, Jon and his partner Michael, with fondness. Michael had been a "naughty boy" on a few occasions and Jon knew it, but Jon was crazily in love with Tim and things, as they say, could easily have happened at any given time. Jon made it clear he wanted uncontrolled, full-on sex with Tim and declared his love, but Tim was in a difficult situation and refused. The last time Tim heard from Jon was when Tim and his then partner received an invite to Jon's marriage to a girl who was a nurse.

It was to be a grand occasion. They hired top hats and tailcoats and looked just like all the other gentlemen on the day. No one passed comments. The bride was happy, and the best man was a friend who was known to all as the "Iron Maiden." Tim has often wondered! Times change, and so do people.

Jon made no secret of his background. Jon's father was a well-known industrialist in the city, but due to certain circumstances Jon lived away from the Hampton family home, to fulfil his own life and ambitions.

Perhaps that was the reason Jon preferred to live as he did, and as so many did, in a flat with someone he looked after and was loved by in return. Suddenly, Jon didn't find that, nor that abounding love, with Michael.

Hearing of so many men who married for similar reasons, one hopes Jon's change of heart brought him that responsibility that was so shunned for so many years, but the cravings, the desires ... was it so easy to dispel? It seems that your price to pay for a life of deep intrigue and dissent, and to bring children into such a situation, could not have been easy. A pretence ... A yearning, almost, for that which had been enjoyed and such a part of one's life — to try and cast to one side could not have been as easy as hoped.

# 1967 Sexual Offences Act – No Longer Illegal

The 1967 Sexual Offences Act was welcomed by gay men across the world, without a doubt but, as with all changes, some will always abuse it and, as I said earlier, for passion. To love the journey must, and does, change. The living together, making a good home, and sharing was so much easier. But it didn't change everything overnight, and nor will it. No one in the world can change a person's feelings with the swipe of a pen. There will always be bigots and it is the totally decent man or woman who recognises this even now … and why? Because they are being let down by generation who cares not a whit for the preceding years.

Because of changes in laws, etc., so much is possible. Open for debate maybe, but possible, single, decent, respectable young men are now allowed to adopt children as a single parent. Two men who are openly gay and living together as a couple have the same advantage, offering unwanted children the opportunity to make good in life and achieve with the support of loving parents. How good must that feel? Of course, there will be raised eyebrows, and of course, there will be questions and narrow-mindedness, but let there be no question that love is everywhere and everything is possible.

But was it all for good? There remain to this day differing opinions, there have to be. In the day, in the moment we live in, there are many good, kind men and woman trapped in marriages into which they should have never entered, but did so to satisfy tradition and family status, simply afraid of being branded as "one of them."

It almost seems ridiculous to write, as it seems we are talking of hundreds of years ago – and yes, it does go back that far – for celebrities of yesteryear are now making their decisions to be known as gay to the world; so too are guys who have always known and suppressed their feelings because of ridicule. Sports men and woman, police officers, vicars and clergy of all denominations are now declaring "I was afraid to tell, so I married." Is that not the sin?

## Living Together – But Something Missing?

Tim and Chris had now been together for several years, and Chris continued to work nights. However, Tim started to feel spending five nights, and latterly, more likely seven nights a week alone watching TV was becoming lonely. No romantic moments; even the occasional event of mutual pleasure, sadly, had now become non-existent. Tim wanted more than being friends. Chris knew of the surgical operation Tim had undergone several years earlier and successfully tried penetration, thinking that this was the way forward now, with Tim's partner's encouragement and care. Sex continued to be non-existent, and on the occasions when Chris was aroused, and Tim was hopeful, Chris did as so many men do … "did it himself" and went to sleep.

By now Tim was aware "the gym" was possibly calling, as Chris started wandering and spending more and more time "at the gym." The inevitable eventually happened after Tim and Chris were together six years. Tim, so much frightened and saddened, lost everything again.

It wasn't a happy parting and that "gentleman," Chris, turned into a bully, knocking Tim about in a temper before introducing his newfound love to Tim … So, Tim's concerns ended up being well founded, as the gym had definitely been calling.

The sad thing is, even people who Tim thought of as friends had an opinion, despite never asking to be told what really happened, and supposedly intelligent professional men acted, and still do in these later years, behave like washerwomen gossiping. It doesn't help, it deeply hurts, but that's life all over.

## As One Door Closes ... Another Mysteriously Opens

When Tim and Chris split up, Tim was sad; he had lost everything again.

But it wasn't all bad; several months before Tim and Chris parted, Tim had reason to go to the bank for the company he worked for. As he walked there, Tim had noticed a guy working on a building site who made his intentions very clear, but Tim really wasn't interested, so just passed him by. However, on one of Tim's trips to the bank, the guy working on the building site made it his business to follow Tim and was doing the same as Tim, turning back to look over his shoulder, ignoring passers-by but keeping an eye on Tim. Turning around the corner they were both aware of each other. After half an hour Tim returned to the shop and was trying to act as normal as possible, but then he looked through the window and saw the same guy, smiling back at him.

Before Tim knew it, they were outside, agreeing to meet later that evening. As per usual, Chris was on duty that evening, leaving Tim feeling lonely and unwanted and at the same time intrigued about what the evening could hold.

## The Evening That Changed Tim's Life – Forever!

Tim kept looking at his watch; it was getting closer to the time they agreed to meet. Tim's heart beating faster and faster ... suddenly there was a knock at the door.

Within no time at all they were in each other's arms, naked and enjoying all that had been hidden by his new friend's blue jeans when they had talked earlier, and the mass of hair which had peeped through his open-neck shirt certainly went a great deal further, which turned Tim on even more ... That grand moment had arrived and all was good! It had to be their secret, for there were other people involved who had no idea of any of this.

After their first encounter, the meetings became frequent, and they enjoyed every moment they shared. The intimacy they shared was what it should be: warm, tender, and gentle, always ending with caring passionate arms that said love so simply.

It had its difficulties; of course it did. Tim had never done anything like this before and was fiercely guilty. Remember, as of this point in time Tim and Chris remained together, and Chris totally unaware of Tim's recent encounters.

Tim's new "friend" had learned of Tim's love of flowers and would quite regularly arrive with an enormous bunch of blooms. Where was Tim to put them? How to explain from whence they came? In a way, Tim was lucky; their meetings were in the autumn and the flowers were mainly chrysanthemums. Tim resolved the problem by removing all the wrapping, cellophane, ribbons etc. and wrapping them in newspaper so that when Tim arrived home he could declare, "The man who grows chrysanthemums has brought some more in … Look! Don't they look lovely?" to which Chris replied, "Yes, they certainly do."

It was telling lies, it was deceit, and it was on the road to heartbreak – but was it the lonely life that was coming to an end for Tim?

Tim found himself in love! … Not only was he in love with the "chrysanthemum man," he was receiving the love he always wanted, dreamed of and waited for – a sexual love. And why shouldn't he? Just because he found love with another man?

To be told he looked nice, to be told his smelled nice when he wore his favourite Estee Lauder perfume, which he had worn for all time, not just be noticed, but to also feel good when the chips were down; at last Tim had found someone he felt could be a future "partner," where their feelings, love, and care for each other were reciprocal. The two went hand in hand.

There's a saying, "from humble beginnings," and that certainly was the case here, for this story will go on to tell of the florist shops Tim and his "chrysanthemum man" would end up owning jointly in later years.

# Breaking Up Is Hard to Do …

Tim and Chris were together through all the trials and tribulations that life had brought, but life goes on … and despite the changes that life brings, there was, so naturally, contentment, age, sharing, and working together.

However, when Tim and Chris parted it wasn't as anyone would have wished, it came about because, as in so many relationships, heterosexual or gay, it was simply a case of someone who knew the secrets they were living under and made it their business to inform the other parties concerned. However, there's a but, and it always is a big but, they themselves knew their own situation best; however, a little more added to the real situation makes it ten times worse.

Tim was not proud of the situation –he was a "let's talk it over" person. To be physically attacked and left bloodied and bleeding, as well as in pain, was a shock in itself, but it must be remembered in fairness that when that took place there were only two people present and only one person saw the damaged body … still, the exaggeration added to the truth caused more than enough pain.

However, they do say out of evil comes good, and in all situations as human beings we have to move on.

# CHAPTER 5

# 1970s: Approaching & "Coming Out"

## Living in the Closet – Gay Underworld

Gay men had their own meeting places, just as they did before the change in the law. They would gather in places they called "Molly houses" where they could socialise, dress as women, have sex and do all the things guys do.

It is even recalled that one vicar was well known for conducting marriages of same sex people. As far back as 1822 a Bishop whose job it was to sort out these goings on was caught in the act of "getting his leg over" with a soldier … how much has changed? Very little, it seems, apart from law changes.

Though many of us have memories that stretch back further than the current generations would welcome, or wish, maybe age does NOT have something to do with attitudes. It has to be said the basic reality is that homosexuality is never going to disappear from life and all it is. Men will always love men and women will always love women … It's not a sin, or a name some would want to give it, simply because it is different to what they understand, or accept, as normal.

There, that strange misuse of an often debated word, wasn't meant to depict all the people, all the situations, all the memories that have been mentioned in this book; they are truly normal in every sense, and I hope whoever reads this book will really believe that.

# Where to Meet On a Saturday Night – Being Gay – Before Nightclubs Appeared?

The 1970s seems to have claimed so much notoriety in what became the gay scenes. It is ridiculous to imagine that prior to that era there were not pubs and clubs that were inhibited by the "queers" of the day. They were in every town, city and yes, made a lot of money for their owners!

## Saturday Night – "Boys'" Night Out

What memories there are of a bus, an ordinary red service bus, fulfilling its duty between one town and another on a Saturday night, taking its passengers to where ever they need to go … one might say manly people, couples on a night out, singles going to meet friends for a drink, and oh my goodness! "Them" … the queers … all heading for the bar in the town where they would be sure of meeting friends in a discreet environment, where no one was a stranger. When the bus driver called the name of the pub you knew, he knew where you were going and had no problem; after all, this is where his load lightened.

You didn't want to walk with a swagger, this was a residential area. People knew how to behave, people didn't want telling where you were going, they guessed. As long as they didn't bring disrespect to the pub or the area, it was ok.

## Aunty to Everyone

Of course, Tim is remembering "Aunty's" at Walsall, so called because the old lady licensee had seen so many generations come through her doors that she was simply "Aunty" to everyone who entered. If she liked you, and the way you behaved, you were always welcome.

From the minute you walked in the door, you were greeted and felt happy. Why wouldn't you ? You were among friends. The shiny chrome fittings, the fashionably garish walls weren't thought about; it was the atmosphere that was important. Occasionally someone would walk in and all eyes would discreetly look when someone said the name of a well-known star, or what is now called a celebrity. They all knew Aunty's, they all knew they were safe!

And when time was called, there was always a party to be invited to, if you so wished!

But don't forget the shop on the outskirts of Birmingham, whose owners had an extension built on the back where dozens of guys would descend and dance and drink the hours away. But there was no harm, no noisiness, or attention seeking. They were there to enjoy the company, and you did.

Like dozens of other situations, you thought nothing of walking home, sometimes miles in the early hours. You wouldn't do that today, or even think of it, it's just not safe today (and would those today who are in their late teens/early twenties ever think of walking anywhere, let alone a mile or even a few miles?).

So often in these pages, it's worth remembering those who died and fought for their fair play that makes today so different, and you realise that the world, or at least where you live, still sees you as … "different," although they don't say it, and as the old saying goes: "As you sow, so shall you reap."

When we speak of the young men prior to the big change, who would have been subject to questions from parents with regard to friends, venues etc., it was easy to tell untruths and cover for one another, knowing the consequence if found out.

## A Tolerant Police Force

Let it not be forgotten that even in these times policemen, and it was basically policemen in the force, were discreet and tolerant.

Recalling the parties where thirty or more guys would be dancing, snogging, smooching, call it what you will – there was nothing bad going on as represented in today's films, they were just human beings letting their hair down – and then a knock would come on the door. Suffice to say, the house emptied, and the garden became busy! Every shrub, every tree, every shed etc. became a shield for some god-fearing guy simply having a night out with his mates.

Opening the door there would be one, two, or even three (burly to the rest of us) policemen, capable of throwing the guys into the back of a van single handed, standing there saying simply, "Keep the noise down lads, enjoy yourselves," adding knowingly, "we've had a complaint … Goodnight." The door closed and everyone returned to what they were doing before, whatever that was!

## Remaining "Sweet, Innocent and Ignorant"

Many times before, when he makes it known that he was one of the thousand men who completed a two-year term of National Service in the Army, he has heard the tales told by so many a gay man about their experiences whilst in the forces, and their surprise that Tim had come through without being involved in anything like that at all. It was true and he just wanted to be believed … for at the time it was the early 1950s, after all.

Tim spoke, earlier, of his colleague, the chef who called him darling – looking back, he was a nice-looking, well-presented guy, swarthy and with a darker skin and a small dark moustache, but he never made any unwanted moves and was obviously more experienced and acquainted with life than Tim.

Tim was innocent and ignorant on such matters; he really hadn't thought of anything like that and truly thought it was just how the chef talked and interacted with everyone.

Reflecting, further back, to his school days, perhaps the closeness of school pals was the only time, and that was only because his pals always treated him decently. It was something that Tim valued. Each one seemed to treat Tim with respect and Tim always felt special when they said they would call for him when making arrangements to meet.

There was one special lad who always wanted to walk to school with Tim and or lookout for him. Tim thought that was nice, but nothing more; although Tim had been aware, and times had been different, who knows what may have happened?

When any one of them called for Tim, and they differently did overtime, Tim knew he felt like the cat that he got the cream … Like a girl waiting for a boyfriend, is probably the way to put it.

## Being Selective in Choosing Friends

Anyway, through early adulthood was the same; mates were always well chosen, never the "ruffs & scruffs" for Tim. When Tim thinks about it, he had always plumped for nice guys, and work colleagues too.

In thinking of his days as a furniture salesman, a guy at one of the other branches would ring and ask Tim if he was going to the annual dinner and dance. Tim didn't think so, for he didn't like that sort of thing. Still, the guy kept asking and Tim kept refusing, and finally he accepted he was getting nowhere.

But then he started asking Tim to meet him for a drink, but they didn't, so it was nothing physical. It was from there that Tim went into national service, so they never had any more contact, but Tim never forgot his name and of course wonders what happened to him.

## The Law Changed in 1967 –
## But Was Society's Attitude Also Changed?

When one talks about the men and women who were affected by the legality of homosexuality, everyone knew someone who remained single, perhaps at home with a parent, mother or father, after the loss of the other. After all, they were family, they were friends, they were neighbours; nothing was strange or different about them. They were treated as such, they would cook, clean, keep their home nice, go shopping … in fact, all those things that come naturally, but maybe everyone did feel something was not quite the same.

Whether it was the law that prevented them from mixing or the fear of it, one will never know!

Because of the severity of being found guilty, folk maintained that live and let live was the right thing. One never heard about school friends, or the likes, having ever been approached by someone, but it obviously happened … hence the law then. As now public toilets were, and always have been, a magnet for illicit sex adventures, modernisation calls are made for these to be closed down, or put out of action on a daily basis, with the reason of costs being given.

But, as in all things, as one door closes, another opens. As much as attempts are made to stop crimes of this nature, the core of those desirous to follow the criminal offenses will always find a way, without thought or regret.

If this is the case let us hope, and pray, genuinely pray, that the younger generation coming up behind us will understand the seriousness of the advice given by older generations.

Clothes and money were less accessible and so were valued more by the individual – pride in oneself. Naturally, everyone was not the same; conditions of life, the way it was lived differ, now as then, one to another. But when laws changed, did everything else change?

## Living Accommodation – Also Required Discretion

To portray gay men living in what is known today as multi-occupied accommodation would certainly have been frowned upon, what a giveaway. Young single men of days gone by were more likely to have rented a room as a flat or bedsitter in a large house, usually under the supervision of an understanding landlord under the strict instructions, "no girlfriends." The youth of today, often featured in films, TV, etc., who are portrayed as having multiple, open sexual interactions might be an imagination of the writer to some extent, but the titillation it provides for some is belief for many others; or maybe this is a prediction of the expected.

## Neighbours next door – Gay relationships extend to 2 woman also

Growing up, Tim, like many folk, had been aware of two women living together because, as it was put then, they were "sisters." They were good friends and so on, so very different back then, and this was of course before the laws of equality; ladies were ladies and a nice, neat home was a natural expectation. They were so nicely dressed and held jobs that encouraged the genteel side of nature. Again, there were exceptions – always the finger pointing at the manly haircuts, and to see a female wearing trousers was sure to raise eyebrows. But they did it because that was not natural to the individual.

Again, laws changed and the modern-day lady became somewhat different, presenting themselves as their hearts desired, but may be not as discreet as their forebears.

Tim recalling the "two ladies", who had been their neighbours for many years, they were "*devoted sisters*", was how they described themselves. One had family similarities, the other didn't, it was a joke; but you know, whoever we are, wherever we go in this world, and whatever our standing is in this life, regrettably, someone always pops up and says, "Oh, you must be so and so, who lived in such and such a place, and your family … lived on pretence." Someone always knows our background!

These two ladies had lived in the street for many years, and so had most of the neighbours. They were aware the boys were gay, and perhaps in some small way were afraid they may be outed, but they forgot, it seems, that local people knew the family history far more than was wanted or expected as a talking point. People can be very discreet, and you know there is always one old lady who knows them better than they know themselves, and loves to tell people about "those nice young men at number … (gay guys!)"


## Neighbourly Love – Expectations Shattered

The neighbour on the other side to Tim was totally opposite to the two lovely "sisters." Tim wasn't a wimp; by this time in his life he had been in the army, he worked in factory environment, and he had heard all the swear words. What he hadn't experienced was females who portrayed themselves to the world as intelligent, well dressed women, holding good jobs, calling some of the filthiest names across the garden fence, using the "F-word" and several others to describe their gay neighbours who, upon reflection, put up with it far longer than they should have!

Their comments with regard to the neighbours, Tim and Alf, brought them their own due justice when their outing became their own responsibility. It's been said for years, you know, that there is no battle bigger than a spiteful female and a gay guy.

# Homophobic Attacks Continued

Read again that page that talks about the meaning of the word gay, reflecting the definition found in the oxford dictionary, 30 words or near enough, each with the meaning of the word gay, frivolous but intense, whoever we are, wherever we live, however long we have known we gay. Let us remember those who lost their lives. It wasn't all simple attacks, it was, and still is, murderous attacks on innocent human beings, their Sin: being "queer."

It's no use the "lovely person," the "gentle," "light up the room," etc. Parents can try and believe they understand, in reality they don't. One never knows who is confronting another. We oldies know … don't they know all the answers?

## Even After the 1967 Law Change – Does Behaviour Matter?

Firstly and foremostly you are a male, a man, a youth, a boy, so however effeminate, you think, you behave like one. Experience of the world shows nothing is more irritating than someone who tells the world, "Look at me, I'm a male and I want to be a girl." Don't pitch your voice so you sound like one, no one won medals for impersonation, but do notice people around you when you do these actions … you will be surprised.

For god's sake, remember you are a man. It's that attention you bring to yourself that is not clever, it may attract the wrong person. Just be the nice manly gay. There is no crime in that. Too many have been murdered for pretending.

Passion is passion whoever, whatever, is involved. Actions, words, feelings that are deep down within are expressed as part of these tender moments, as most people know, and for years, nature being what it is, just as passion was being aroused and the intenseness of two naked bodies working together in ecstasy, came the words "marry me." For years the impossibility only led to the real loving reason for these words. Tim himself knew what all this was about, he experienced it, and of course so had thousands of many men, over many years. It's true, women too, but all eyes were focused on men.

## How Society Perceived a Gay Person – The Stereotypical Description

In films, stories, etc., homosexuals were always, without fail, played as a poofs, very effeminate men, and the definition of the word gay sums that up perfectly.

In the far-off days when men wore wigs etc. for vanity reasons, that was accepted in all its forms, but modern history portrays gays as all types of men, from train drivers to hairdressers, boilermen to bakers, and that seems very fair, for the hiding (thankfully) has gone.

Tim himself discloses in these memories that he, for a while, experienced all kind of work, most of which he enjoyed and learned a great deal from, and of course, the colleagues who he worked with, and sometimes their views on the gay world! That tells its own stories, one of which Tim shares with the reader.

On leaving school he joined what was then the GPO (the General Post Office), now renamed Royal Mail, as a messenger boy, riding a bicycle around the town and its suburbs, delivering telegrams of messages of great importance, long before what today one takes for granted … the internet and email communication. Tim worked in offices and sometimes had contact with the shop floor workers. Nice clean jobs, so many conditions that wouldn't be tolerated in this day and age.

Then a shop manager, window dresser, which for some reason was reputed to tell the whole world you were gay, oh, and yes, even a bus conductor. That was where Tim met the first "tranny" in his life, a big burly guy who wore so much makeup it was false, and his navy blue uniform jacket held a film of face powder. Although this was in the early 60s, he got away with it; a few titters here and there, especially when he shouted, in a very deep male voice, "upstairs only please."

But from each other one learns something that makes Tim the person he is today, meeting all kinds of people with the compassion and understanding for most.

## Dad Being So Proud – A Big Surprise

For many years, Tim didn't understand why he worked for a company where his dad also was employed, albeit on the factory floor; it was a huge learning curve that most gays will understand. Notoriously the latter will always claim to have been at odds with their father for whatever reason, no one seems to know. Tim was no different, perhaps harking back to his early childhood previously mentioned.

Like all people of his age, Tim had many artistic talents and hobbies. It was how we survived the winter nights. It was usual for his mom to show these around to friends and family with pride. Tim's dad would look on from the sidelines with a fatherly look, whatever that meant.

But then this day came when Tim, as part of his job, had to walk around the shop floor where his dad worked. Tim never told anyone of their relationship. They would speak as with any other, but the men and women just guessed, Tim supposed, until one day one of the guys in conversation said, "Your dad is so proud of you, you know."

Tim replied in surprise, "He never tells me that."

The guy said, "Your dad has been telling us all about that and the beautiful wedding cakes you make and all the other things you do."

Shocked, Tim contained his feelings and it was never mentioned again, but from that moment Tim saw his dad in a different way; so much so that Tim was with his dad when he passed away and remained close to him for the ensuing years. He adored him, he was his guardian angel.

## Father & Son Relationship

Many years later, people still ask the same questions about the relationship between gay men and their fathers: Was he good? Was it bad? How did he accept it (the father, that is)? And so on. In reality I suppose men of his father's age would have been through those vile years of persecution for gays.

One's Father would, without a doubt, have recognised a difference between his sons, any father would and does … or maybe not! Being unable to come to terms with his son being gay … maybe there are many reasons!

"Was he unkind to you?" someone asked. "Did he treat you badly?" another said. Gazing into his memories, Tim would simply say, with a lump in his throat and unable to hold back the tears, "I know he was proud of me, as I was of him." I never let him down; of that I'm proud. He was a proud ex–First World War soldier and he taught Tim to walk proud and smart.

The term rough and ready is used elsewhere in these pages, but most lads were respectable and decent; there was no ill treatment in Tim's family.

## Tim and Alcohol – an Alien Mix

Alcohol never held any attraction where Tim was concerned; perhaps folk could jump in and say it was to do with the way Tim saw his brother behave. Who knows, but Tim wasn't interested and never made a secret of it.

Quite recently someone asked if Tim would like a drink and Tim made a joke of it, saying, "I will have a port and lemon." "But that's a lady's drink," came the reply (For Tim, this was a reference to the one and only drink Tim had with his Dad before returning to National Service Training).

## The Carefree 1970s – Being Gay, Being in the Closet – No Longer

This book was written with hope, it was never meant to be for the purpose of titillation and excitement and may be a disappointment to some who lived their lives along that path.

When you have lived a life that is, to some, strangely different, the inspiration is to write and share the realities of how many ways life can be good … just different!

For those who read, and fully understand its contents, the changes that have already been made will be familiar, but do we sit back contented? Or do we hope that more changes will come about in future years bringing forward the fantasies of some, but the realities that the world would never want to see, at any cost?

## Each Generation – A Different Outlook on Life – Different Expectations Drive Changes

Each generation will bring with them their own changes; should they be accepted without discussion and contemplation? … Maybe not, although it is important to consider the points of view from opposition, for we ourselves can be blind when and where necessary. The free and easy approach taken in the 60s & 70s, certainly changed the way gay guys conducted their lives … No longer kept behind closed doors, making their sexuality very public … a change for the better?

## Finally, the Beginning of a Long Lasting & Meaningful Relationship

A new home, a new partner, a new life. As has been said many times, perhaps even in this book, all any of us want in life is love … we find it and want to keep it.

The gay community has always been accused of having been promiscuous, and in many cases it has been warranted. There have been more one-night stands between homosexuals over time than anyone would believe, and it's easy to put blame on the fragility of partnerships onto the way the gays, then and now, lived in fear and secrecy. But not all gays are the same; Tim was not an exclusion. Before AIDS ever existed, there were many who wanted a nice home of their own, with a caring partner to cosy up to. Normal guys look for a female, gays look for that same sex partner, and isn't it true: you never know anyone until you live with them, so who knows how long any relationship will last?

Going back to the years prior to the Sexual Offenses Act 1967, surely the opportunity of getting to know someone was even more difficult, and how could they really know who they were associating with amidst all that secrecy? But it does happen, long term relationships (as Tim & Alf will prove).

## There Needs to Be a Beginning – The Catalyst to Creating More

The quip far back in this book referred to Tim noticing his new partner's chest hair peeping above his T shirt when they talk for the first time and the tight blue jeans all momentarily, but it's surprising what attracts us to any individual! Well, it is, and there has to be a beginning …

Because he was a builder by trade, Alf recently made all the arrangements to complete buying his first house, and was excited to get started altering it. He was happy that Tim was now about to share it with him; it was *their* new home!

There was a lot to do. They both worked full time during the week, and weekends were spent making alterations. It was universally a "do-it-yourself" era. The 70s was a time not only for buying and selling property, but also for making the old look futuristic too. It took a lot of money and was something neither of them had, as once again Tim had found himself the poorer of a broken relationship – you might say "not again!" but yes is the answer! Tim had trusted Chris, and Chris had charge of all finances, so Tim left with nothing when starting this new relationship with Alf.

## 12 Months Later – Determination Wins the Day

But the past is the past, and within the first 12 months the house was looking rather nice, they thought, and unbeknownst to them the local newspaper had been informed of these "two guys and their lovely home."

The reporter came, took photographs, and gave the story in the next edition with the title "Bachelors of Opulence" – it seemed they knew they had achieved something they were proud of and took on completing the task.

Alf was a perfectionist and Tim was pleased to keep the standards high, liveable, but not a show home. They were well accepted by neighbours and soon became part of the group, organising events. It was here they held many parties, of course, for their friends and, on occasions, family too. There were always dinner parties just because …

## Entertaining – So Natural to Tim & Alf

Religion often played a part in the life of gay men and women and around this time they found themselves hosting people from around the country, which they love doing.

At one of the parties, for a birthday, Alf surprised Tim with a black poodle pup, the first of four over the years; life was never the same again, as anyone who has had a dog will tell you. They were living a nice life now, a beautiful home and garden, holidays in Bournemouth and the likes, and a car.

# CHAPTER 6

# 1980s: A New Pandemic? – Generation X

## A Gay Disease – Or Scapegoat?

Although no named individual, for that would not be possible, many of the men referred to herein have left us a legacy. A legacy of daring and fear, which only they could tell us. So too can they, those who in their latter years of life, still suffer the indignities of knowing that, in a moment they probably can't recall, they became a victim, and remain a victim of AIDS, or the associated viruses. They and people like them fell into a situation, like many of us have done, and trusted.

Tim himself is aware of friends who have trusted, only now to find themselves in a position that cannot be changed, but who, thank God, are lucky to be able to benefit from the wonder of modern medicines, enabling them to live with at least some dignity.

The past is gone, there's no point in looking back. Those who escaped were not clever, we're not the chosen ones; we and they are the lucky ones. We know, like everyone else, the overwhelming excitement of an undressed penis, the thrill of wanting "it" in any way possible, and in the heat of the moment, none of us have time for inspection.

For the younger man, let it be known the art of penetration is nothing new; it has always been a part of the sexual fulfilment most sought. Changes in law cannot bring change, that we know, but what they can do is to bring with them the responsibility of caring for each other. The change of the sexuality act did not say "no penetration," how could it? It was to safeguard the community we know as gay, the homosexual community, those that enjoy and need each other. It was to dispel any, or all, clandestine meetings etc., which had been so much a part of the past.

## "The World" Appears to Profess to Be Experts

Despite what is being written and portrayed, the 80s brought more changes than could be imagined, but on the side lines were people who made a living from writing about subjects they were so often not involved with nor qualified to talk about on a personal level; still, they wrote and broadcast what they *thought* they knew.

## The Worlds Reaction to AIDS – "The Gay Disease?"

When AIDS first hit the world news, the homosexual world took on its greatest battle of all time. It started in many countries across the world, not excluding Great Britain. A pandemic bringing fear and, most likely, death, but in somewhat different way than had been known before. This battle involved anyone, anywhere, who indulged in such activities for the sake of being who they were. One wonders, with the onset of this epidemic, if for many years the information had been at hand but simply withheld in a shroud of secrecy? Perhaps having such knowledge to hand provided a "we told you so" attitude. The dramatic effect has been such that it is only in recent days of writing this paragraph that the name of the first victim, the first British man known to have died from AIDS, has been released. Same sex situations were nothing new ... they never were and never will be, despite the changes in the law every few years.

Through all of those years that have been talked about in this book, and others, men have loved men and women loved women, but look back and read again the facts of this; the greater majority of these affairs were based on dignity, pride and a standard of life far beyond any other because of the secrecy and trust that was involved between two people. The fear and injustice afforded to them meant everything; risks were part of who they were.

## Jubilations Post-1967 law change also brought sad memories

With the ultimate freedom given to them by means of a change in law back on July 27, 1967, life and exchanges became easier every day. Remember this, if you will: the jubilations were only partly of joy for some, for life had its memories; it would never be the same in many ways.

A new generation was coming along, several in fact: generations of young men and women who could not, in any way, imagine what had gone before their time, who were not for sorrow, but for a future of doing as they pleased and being whom they wanted to be.

The jubilations for some never existed, how could they? It meant so many thousands of men who had craved that love, whatever their situation, could now involve themselves in a new world, a new life, almost.


## AIDS Versus Carefree Society and Risk Averse

Not saying this new brigade were any less clean or particular, but they were living double lives. They were in sexual relationships with wives, girlfriends and yes, even prostitutes, so who knows?

The little boys, not quite schoolboys, but ordinary everyday youngsters who we have mentioned earlier, were good bait for some men.

Tim recalls a holiday he and his partner had in Morocco and the "availability" of boys, young men, following them around asking for sex.

AIDS had hit the world, and with a vengeance. Condoms became a must-have and a necessity, not a choice as was their history, simply because it prevented the disease being transferred one to another. But were the pundits sure that young boys were as well prepared as their older compatriots? The world was theirs, so to speak; going through those difficult years of their life, experiencing sex in all its forms and with all those people who gave or sold themselves – it was something that was easily accessible.

Prior to these times discretion was not only a requirement, it was the difference between being heard and being seen.

Tim recalls being asked, "Is it an age thing?" Do you know, he couldn't answer one way or the other. Tim recalled his memories of being in pubs or clubs with his friends having a pleasant evening and all of them, most of them, at times calling to the youngsters around the room to keep the noise down and to keep their behaviour in check.

## AIDS – Where Did It Come From?

Even the clever scientists of the day, the doctors etc., were never really able to put a pin on the origins of AIDS.

Until now, and increasingly so in later years, England has been becoming multinational on a grand scheme. But where now are the boys from Morocco, from Egypt or India, who had freely said they wanted to come to England to earn good money? Isn't that why we were not even tempted, as so many may have been before, just two guys on holiday – isn't that what we went on holiday for? Maybe some did, of course … many still do but there are still, perhaps, in this day and age, more who are in good stable relationships.

Now there is evidence of that one soldier in the First World War who is suspected of being the first carrier.

In this world of technology, in all its varying forms, where the history of AIDS is open for all to see read and discuss at length, this book was never meant to deal with such a strong subject in detail; there are far more prolific writers than this one to do that, they who fought causes before the act of parliament and have continued to do so, engaging in their ranks people who are not able to do so. So forgive the writer for not professing to be an expert in the same subject; this book was written with a huge experience and with a vision of how times and people have changed – you, the reader, will decide.

## Experiencing, First Hand, Someone Suffering from AIDS

When Tim owned businesses, he was always looking for staff to complement the reputation of the shops; good young people who were interested in the trade, to help and train. One day a young man came into the shop to make a purchase. Tim moved to serve him, and he became very talkative, and from his expressed knowledge he was clearly interested in floristry. As it was nearing Christmas, he then asked Tim if there were any vacancies. He was obviously gay, he spoke well – both were an asset – and he knew the trade. Tim spoke to his partner, Alf, at home that night and together they agreed it would be a good move to give him a trial.

## A New Member of Staff – Concerns Raised

His name was Ken, mid 20s, and he produced quality work, which was the most essential thing.

All seemed to be good; Ken was amiable and got on well with the female staff. A day off here and there, without prior notice or agreement, was probably the worst thing, with the orders dependent on time and day.

However, the staff were becoming concerned with the amount of telephone calls from a local hospital for Ken and told Tim of their concerns.

One of the staff, a lady with two sons, asked if she could speak to Ken on behalf of the directors and staff, and it was agreed this should take place in an informal manner.

Ken admitted to her that he was having treatment for AIDS, or, shall we say, was supposed to be having treatment. The calls were referring to his non-attendance at hospital. It was agreed he could continue to work, primarily because the girls felt they could keep an eye on him and his hospital treatment, and he did so.

Like so many before and after him in this world, Ken … what is the saying? … bit the hand that fed him.

What happened to staff loyalty and respect for those who offered a helping hand?

Ken cheated, he lied, he stole to buy God knows what, and he continued to flaunt his sexual activities. The time came when enough was enough and something had to be done to curb the fraud and to help the guy himself. The shop was well known for the sale of extremely good quality glass and china, and Ken relieved the manager one day a week whilst the latter had the day off.

It became noticeable that the most expensive item in the shop was always sold on that day … or was it?

The partners and their friend set a trap, out of necessity, to find what was happening, and did so with ease.

David, a lover of all things beautiful (and a trusted friend of Tim and his partner), went into the shop and purchased … that's right … the most expensive piece of cut glass. On leaving the shop David rang Tim to advise him he had done so, but the young man (Ken) regretted that the till was not working.

There being only a short distance between the two shops, Tim was quickly able to confront Ken; of course, he denied it – the customer must have come into the shop whilst he was out the back. There is no glory to this tale. In fact, Tim and partner travelled from address to address, each one of which had been given as Ken's home address, only to find at each one, or several, pieces of the stock which were missing from the shop.

But there is worse to come. During those searches, Tim & his partner met Ken's brother and offered their sympathies on the loss of their father, for only two days after Ken began working at the shop he requested permission to make up a rather large and profitable funeral order, as his Dad had passed away. It was agreed Ken could pay for the flowers "as and when" Ken received payment from the family members. To this day, Ken has never paid for the flowers.

## Attitude to AIDS? – Depends Upon One's Age Group

Ken, being so young, continued his sexual activities for as long as Tim knew his whereabouts; a very reckless attitude for someone diagnosed with AIDS. Sadly, Ken was not the only one who took the view "we are young, it does not apply to us, there is no need to practice safe sex, nor take a responsible approach to one's sexual activities."

This isn't a story to ridicule, this is a true story that shows how deep a pit can go when it's a bad one. Tim and his partner often wonder if Ken was lucky or if he did die of AIDS. It was so prevalent at the time, but then, Ken was one of a new generation! So, when Tim speaks of memories, he has actually been there at the front, so to speak. Ken spoke freely of his conquests; as long as they were well equipped to provide his needs, Ken didn't say no – he was honest in that way. Ken didn't care, all he wanted was sexual penetration and he wasn't alone, but how many more … ?

Oh! To add the final blow, when Tim met Ken's brother the children with him were asked, "How's Grandad?" to which they both replied, "He just gave me this."

## AIDS – The Devastating Impact

Wars and pandemics of various kinds had brought their own problems, and many brilliant young men aspiring to make something of themselves had been killed.

AIDS was and did the same in its own way, but brutally, much more brutally. This was not in hate or violence, but in the simple act of love. It didn't kill just the rich and famous, the names on everyone's tongue, but also ordinary people. It did, and is possibly still likely to, kill those we know as friends, friends of friends, acquaintances, and just ordinary guys, even straight men who dared to explore and investigate.

When people look into the past and are reminded of these times, the reality of the tragedy arises, but has in recent times been compared with modern times. AIDS has as much to do with changing generations as anything else.

Tim remembers the parties, the excitement of the new face in the crowd, and the anxiousness of so many who wanted to tell you that they had had him first, second, or third – but this depiction of the times and activities are either a figment of imagination or a comparison to the writer's youth. They that died mostly have belonged to an era when even an open button on the flies would have been frowned upon. As for anything else sexual, it was considered out of order; you had been invited because you were one of the crowd, you are of the same ilk, and you would not have defiled your friends home.

And as for more recent portrayals in films etc., running about naked before, making a display of the act … again, that fear was always there … what about the knock that would come to the door?

There was bound to be the occasional person who thought this was an opportunity, but this was greatly frowned upon, and in any case suit, collar, tie, etc. got in the way – taking so much time and trouble to make yourself look good put you off taking it off for … a few seconds.

Maybe that is where the dress code changed; young boys didn't wear suits, they thought they looked prettier in vests and the like, to expose themselves to the lecherous older guys. No, these were truly the changing times, the very realisation of freedom gave way to the fact they could, would, and did. Pride in themselves just disappeared with so many of the victims of AIDS in their low teens.

## Another Change – Tim and his Generation Found It Challenging to Accept Being of No Benefit to the Gay Community

Tim and his partner, Alf, had never been at all interested or involved with any pride organisations. There is much to be written on the subject; this is the modern way, like it or not, but we didn't all change overnight. We may still be living in the past – or are we still afraid?

The old myth "my parents don't know" is a joke to the very roots of its origins. Just parade a dozen mothers and ask each of them the question; you will get all kinds of answers, from the polite, mummy mums who will answer, frightfully posh, "I thought there was something different," to the warm homely mum who answers honestly, "every mother knows," and wants only the best as she does for all her children.

You see, they are proud of you and your ambitions, but don't take advantage of their support.

## Maintaining Respect for Your Elders, Including Your Parents

Perhaps, for the older generation, the respect and admiration for Mum is still there and, at the risk of sounding old fashioned, is the one joy to hold onto. Just because a young man, or lady for that matter, becomes part of the gay community, their mother does not simply change to being a mate; the swear words we all know and hear, and which have been avoided purposely in this book, are so familiar in today's world that they are part of a vocabulary for many. To hear them being shared with parents is not clever, but then we have to realize the acceptance of use is modern, but degrading. There was a time when mums would have been treated as the queen in terms of admiration.

# External Appearances Can Be Deceiving – As Tim Discovered

In his memories, Tim has the vision of a member of his own family who married into a family a bit better off than his own. There were five or six siblings; two sisters never married, the others did, and so did the brothers, except for one, of whom it was said he remained single so that he could look after his sisters. There had been an occasion where they had been introduced, but had not had a conversation as such until they bumped into each other in a gay bar!

You may think he spoke in the posh voice Tim was expecting him to, but no, he was quite rough and ready when he asked him the question he had obviously asked so many others before him: "Do you like this? You can have it?" (What would Mummy have said?)

Of course mums know, and how are they feeling when they see, on one of the many floats making up the "Pride parade", *their* boy, running about in next to nothing, hanging off a lorry, parading what she had tenderly cared for.

In the gay community, generations have changed so much. In years gone by, guys would have had their own way of showing respect for each other; yes they laughed, they joked, and called each other by names (remember the two on the ship?), but it was all light hearted – they were still homosexuals, you might say trying to be something that they weren't, but aiming to be so much nicer people.

If we're trying to impersonate, let's do it with style. This is the generation that changed so much, for forgetting the past so easily and for all those mums who have said so deeply and inwardly, "Oh, they're only enjoying themselves, but I wish he wasn't. I really would like him to find a nice lad to settle down with," but a dream it would have been for the mothers of long ago to have even been able to make such a wish.

## As the Law Changes – There Are Other "Changes" Too!

Imagine how many children are born and show signs of being different, boys playing with dolls, and girls were doing whatever the boys should be doing, and being rushed off to have sex changes. Do they have a chance or mothers to readily fulfil their child's desire – or their own, in many cases.

I and many others were different, but the little girl thing was never pursued. It couldn't be in those days; you were what your birth certificate said you were and you grew up being "queer." There were no benefits in those days to pay for such surgery.

How many of these boys who were subjected to change will one day, when confronted with an erect penis in the midst of lovemaking, reflect and perhaps think *that could have been me!* … The world turned upside down?

But just one mother's actions is one too many for those who hastily quote the Bible … "Thy will be done on earth.." etc. Yes! We are mostly good living people, you know!

## Reflecting on an Ever-changing World

Looking back as he had been doing, Tim realised the changes that had taken place in his life, the challenges, the fears, the risks, and the escapades which could easily have ended quite differently.

Tim had realised that with all that he recalled as his life, which yes, must have been difficult at times, on a personal level, his own fears were nothing like as bad as they had been in the years prior because of love, a genuine love between two people who happened to care and wanted to share.

Wasn't the fact about the two notorious pubs in the centre of Birmingham mentioned earlier enough to make some scared? Of course it was, wasn't there always a chance of the place being raided? Yes to that, but even in Tim's earlier years, wasn't there the little group of guys who would commandeer certain corners of the pub and share each other's makeup, calling each other girly names?

Pushing the boundaries, some might say, but men were still being arrested for behaving in that way and a smart suit, collar & tie would have provided no defence at all.

So, when the law was changed, hope for good was seen by the majority, and it was. But when it said that the 1980s changed everything, well it did to some extent, but was it as predicted?

To some the gay world was turned on its feet, gone the fear and ridicule, but the privacy and simplicity of lives had gone too. No doubt it's the choice of some, to be honest, to be flamboyant, thinking they're more female than male and, to some, more than was imaginable.

## Acting Camp – For What Benefit?

But were/are the public, the average man and woman in the street, ready for this showing off? "Camp" is the word by which many oldies know it. To be camp is/was not a good thing, it meant you were being too open and was shunned by the gay world for many years.

For many a long year Tim had come through an era where man was man and woman was woman, however one acted. It wasn't a case of what you did in the bedroom, or out of it for that matter.

The gay community of today should give thanks to their predecessors for the understanding and sympathy they earned by being discreet, but to wiggle and pretend to this day only brings an unhealthy embarrassment to the fall.

The 80s dispensed with the nicely dressed look they were so used to, and in came the tight trouser which didn't belie a thing! Large or larger, it was all on show; the technique of dress to impress had gone for good.

Straight or gay, male or female, black or white, whatever, we were born, it seems, with a certain trait in mind to find a mate, a partner, someone who will be destined to share our life. However long, or short a time it may be for, we don't seem to have particular requirements as far as that is concerned. But looking back over the years we can, and do, notice the similar or dissimilar people with whom we have shared any particular space of time with, from school days into adulthood … It's not unusual to say we have strayed off a given, or natural, path and have often found ourselves on an entirely different path to what we may have expected.

To many it's the socializing, active partying scene that seems to attract. Most men seem to follow the trend of being interested in sport because of their own egotistical belief that it's the most important part of being who they are. How strange their interest in the players, too! Their idolising changes their lives, alongside puberty and women, of course. Along the way it seems the strangest of things, situations, make us sit up, take a deep breath and think!


## Footballers – Too – Coming Out

You will recall at the very beginning of this book Tim was wondering why he had suddenly become aware of the closeness of footballers, players, the guys. Of course, he hadn't suddenly become aware; there had never been a time in his life, as he now recalls, when he hadn't wondered about the closeness of those hugs and if perhaps there was something about those moments that would have given room for thought of the nearness. The shorts the players wear were never made of several layers of thick material, so it's only natural they would feel things … but then, they would say "we're all blokes together and no one takes any notice." Were there no closeted gays in all those years? Large or small? Black or white? But we shouldn't forget we have moved on, or, suffice to say, some footballers have. They themselves are now "coming out" and declaring they are gay, and why shouldn't they?

Footballers, sportsmen, being gay, there can't be anything new about that; but just imagine in the days of homosexuality being illegal, when some guy rubbed against you in celebration, did they not sense arousal? Come to think of it, were the people who made the laws blind to the fact this would, could, and did happen? Maybe such things were not talked, much less thought about, or was it the type of stuff for queers only?

Tim remembered when he was working as a shop manager and just around the corner his friend, Ivan, managed a menswear shop. Through both being gay they had known each other for many years.

## The Secrets "Closed Doors" Could Tell

In the quieter times of business, they would go round to each other's shop for a gossip; they had few secrets. Such was the situation that Ivan would ring Tim informing him it wasn't the right time for a chat, and that usually meant he was "entertaining" — and that could mean anything, or anyone, from customers who were looking for more than having an inside leg measured, to any members of the local football team who were looking for discrete time with Ivan, guys who would walk into his shop in glory and whose names could be in headlines the same day for their ability and achievements!

Tim smiles when he hears the names mentioned as "one of the best," but who knows how complicated their lives must have been; the footballer knew his secret was safe.

How many more were there? You will of course remember that this was both before and after the law changed.

Obviously, we didn't all work in gents' outfitters, but there were those moments for all men who showed signs of being gay.

Tim shares his memories of when he was working in the shop around the corner, as he recalls the "naughties" that might have gone on between the "paint and wallpapers."

# What Was the Customer Really Looking For?

In particular, Tim recalls, when working in the paint & wallpaper shop, a very smart young man who came in on one occasion to look through the pattern books of a rather exclusive wallpaper company. These were displayed in a very prestigious showroom, and it was Tim's job as manager to show these to, and advise, the customer.

After the initial discussion with regards to the customer's requirements, it was Tim's task to show the customer what he thought may be suitable. As time went by, the young man introduced himself by name and said that he was a doctor at a local hospital and had bought his first house nearby.

Coffee was served by one of the female staff, who disclosed afterwards that she thought he was getting rather comfortable and looked as if he was going to be looking at wallpaper for some time, as often happened with this sort of customer – stylish, but not necessarily gay. He was, by now, talkative with the staff and seemed to be quite comfortable, and then it was time for the shop to close for lunch.

On reopening after the lunch break, the first customer through the door was … the doctor. Although he had invited Tim to join him for lunch, which was declined, Tim noticed the Doctor now seemed a little more smiley, conversational, friendly, and yes, giggly.

Several comments were made by the staff, to maybe hand over to one of them; it was obviously going to be a very good sale and Tim had other work to do, but the doctor wouldn't hear of it! Tim was convinced that the doctor had his eye on the younger female member of staff and was just wasting time, or did the doctor think he was special, having the manager's attention, as sometimes happened. The staff left them to continue.

It was when the guy asked to use the toilet and stood up … that Tim realised the girls may be right, the doctor did want the manager's attention, but not as Tim envisaged. Tim quickly offered a piece of sample material to cover up the doctor's "rising temperature," to put it politely.

There hadn't been any reason to suspect the doctor's behaviour until now, but there it was … in all its glory. Having been directed to the toilet and returned, the doctor was re-seated and he started getting more embarrassed, knowing what he was trying to hide.

It was time for the doctor to make decisions and plans for his new home. He wrote out the cheque, which was a very substantial amount, so the time Tim had spent assisting the doctor hadn't been wasted, and he certainly enjoyed his lunch, even if the "afters" were disappointing. The doctor left the store, making sure his address was on the reverse of the cheque, as was a customary requirement.

Closing time came and Tim cashed up the tills, counting the change, the notes, and the cheques with the cashier. It was she who noticed, "This one hasn't been signed."

Tim's heart sank and his thoughts went into overdrive … was it a con? Was it a genuine mistake? After all, the doctor was a little, no, a lot, inebriated when he left, and he did have a problem to deal with!

There was only one way to resolve it, to go to the doctor's address … if it existed. Tim's partner at the time agreed to go with him.

A knock on the door, ring on the bell with no answer … was it a wasted journey? But a few more tries, and the door opened, with only a rear room light for illumination. Was Tim surprised with what confronted him? He wasn't sure. He was taken aback when he heard himself saying, "I've got this for you," in a mumble, holding out the cheque, and a voice saying back to Tim, "I'm glad you came, I've been waiting with this … "

Totally naked and condom already in place, he was beckoning for Tim to enter the house … … and then the interior light of the car went on. The cheque was signed, and the door shut. If nothing else, this was yet another learning experience, in many ways.

Gays were as much a part of the community as anything, or anyone else. It could be said, and many did, "Why didn't you grab it?" "Why didn't you go for it? I would have done," or "I'd have grabbed it with both hands … and you mean to say you just ignored it?" … Well, for many those are the most natural reactions, but you know, we're all made differently.

## Being Homosexual, Queer, Or Is the Modern Term Gay?

The reference at the beginning the book with regards to his brother's feelings towards him was not so unusual … when you think that was in the years of homosexuals being queer, that word so freely used in those days, among many of course – pansy, effeminate, there were many more, always have been and always will be, it's pretty certain to say. But then, times change, as they have already done, providing in history some of the finest, most gifted men and women who gave so much to life itself …

It's difficult to put an exact date on when the word gay became fashionable, so to speak. Looking in the dictionary the definition of the word is pretty well self-explanatory. Simple, joyous, lively, colourful, homosexual; one would think a fair description of anyone we know to be gay.

Despite not being the traditional, "normal" heterosexual, the majority of those carrying the nickname do, on a whole, seem to be lively, happy and colourful, and happily live on a "devil may care" vibration; and there is their own acceptance of life and the world. Throughout the years they have cautiously accepted the snares … but with the passing of times, the changes in the law, and in general the changes in attitudes, why, even a change of description of words in dictionaries (look again at the word gay! is it a coincidence that three words now become 32! Bright, brilliant, dashing, fine, showy, flashy, garish, candy, littering, loud, tinsel, blight, cheerful, festive, frivolous, frolicsome, cheerful, festive, gladsome, gleeful, hilarious, jaunty, jovial, light-hearted, and so many more) the world has changed, but the guys are still doing the same thing they have always done, falling in love, sleeping in the same bed, having deep meaningful sex and sharing a love beyond imagination.

Among the many names used, there is not a word the gays of today should leave out, and let us be sure; neither would our forebears, who were persecuted or died of AIDS.

## And the Word "Drag?"

However the word drag became such a part of the gay environment. No one really knows but some say that in the early 60s it set itself alongside the name given to those who were a little louder than most, and was more or less a term of endearment.

The man in any relationship was always referred to as butch, had male instincts and was capable of doing the manly things in all situations.

Younger or older, his partner was the queen, for obvious reasons … "She" wanted to be "cosseted" and, in finding a partner, expect to be treated with respect. As mentioned before, usually, a gay love match is a union of meaningful words. Of course, most couples, gay or straight, have fun; I reached a point of certainty on their lives. Perhaps the reason with the gays is the uncertainty, and the fear of the past, when even having reached it nothing was certain, and anything could have happened. The combination of the two words is quite natural and obvious. "Drag Queens" says it all.

## Drag Acts – Popularity Increases – Many Household Names Established

Dressing up has been with us forever; fun times, parties, theatre, pantomime etc. Men have always dressed in women's clothes, mainly for fun reasons, and of course for their own personal ones too, but it didn't have to be because they saw themselves in that role.

Today's fake females take it all so seriously, if allowed, and wanting to be the latest top line female artist it is good when the audience is laughing with you, but remember this: the comments after can sometimes make you weep.

Perhaps the greatest truth in this is in the Shirley Bassey era. Despite the beer bellies, the beards of all shapes and sizes, moustaches etc., men would put on the prettiest dress, wave their arms about, and pretend, or even believe, that they were indeed Shirley Bassey!

Although a female dressing as man was not unusual; as a soldier or a Prince, Dandini in pantomime; even the old Music Hall star Burlington Bertie from Bo was portrayed by a female.

The rags and tatty costumes of Bessie the Cook in many pantomimes, though carefully created by a man, could not be made to look glamorous for fear of offending or giving the wrong impression – until along came an army of comedians daring to impersonate the female. The list of names is endless, each known for their own styles; glamorous, elegant, blonde, brunette, or as in Tim's style, "the woman at the bus stop, with all the local gossip" – Mrs Shufflewick, who was loved by all.

They weren't necessarily all "batting for the other side," as it was delicately known; at least, they tried to convince us.

Some left doubt in people's minds and others made their name and money by having the wardrobe mistress in charge of their clothes exclusively.

Think for a moment, of their names: Les Dawson, Billy Dainty, Dick Emery, and of course, Danny La Rue. All brilliant, but never a bad word out of their mouths.

It would be foolish to think or believe that older men of yesteryears were not attracted to the "chickens," as they were called, the young boys who, like today's youth, were aware of their sexuality at a very early age, but this world has changed, and the people in it too. Behaviours changed, discipline conforming to society changed, and respect also (some may say non-existent, even).

# Business Expansion – All Going Well

As the years went by times changed of course, and so did Tim's &
Alf retail business; the two flower shops becoming well estab-
lished, a reputation created in the community for their quality,
friendly & reliable service. The business was "blooming" and
the 80s seemed good years for them, despite the old phrase "it
will never last."

# CHAPTER 7

# 1990s: Overseas Holidays

## The Influence of "Mama & Patsy" Returns

When references were made earlier in the book about dressing up in drag, as the gay world knows it, and the reoccurrence of Mama & Patsy, it was meant to be fun, an accepted part of life for many of us who have been involved at some point; it certainly was not meant to infer that most guys like putting on women's clothes! ... Yes, of course there are many men who find some pleasure in it, but many, like Tim has already said, do so for a laugh, to give pleasure to others in a fun way.

## Not Just a Housewarming Party

Tim recalls that when he and Alf first got together, they had worked hard to make their new home presentable and decided, as many do, to give a housewarming party for their friends. Arrangements were made, invites sent out, trying to include as many of their close friends as possible. At these times there always seems to be people who you would like to invite, but would they come? Was it worth trying?

Alf had friends he often spoke of but hadn't seen for years, but let's try them! Tim, being in charge of that side of things, phoned them ... they would love to come, though they lived in Bristol.

## Hidden Talent – Tim Reveals his Alternative Side?

As time went by, there were many conversations between them; in particular one who said the friends in Bristol had much experience in putting on shows for small events and would do so for the planned party, on the condition that Tim took part also! That was a shock for Tim, for he had never done anything like that, but after a lot of persuasion he agreed.

The party came and went, a very enjoyable evening …

## A Gay Partnership Creating So Much Happiness for So Many, Regardless of Sexuality

… But from there onwards was a new story, for the four of them formed a cabaret group. At first, Tim was hesitant and then coerced, or invited, whichever way you put it, to join in and take a tour with a group of likeminded friends to entertain groups of older people at charity dos and venues to raise money for good causes.

The cabaret group performed in front of many, bringing considerable fun and laughter; so much so that when the friends decided to emigrate to Australia, Tim found himself as a solo artist, in demand at clubs and pubs near and far.

## Now Tim's Turn to Entertain – Solo

There was no seriousness about it, and as it was said earlier, off with the costumes off with the pretence. In all those times Tim had said "No gay clubs!" for his own reasons – he didn't want a reputation as a drag queen – but it so happened that one of the calls he got was from a gay club. The club, Tim knew, was well run and conducted and he and his partner had been there many times, so they agreed to do the spot as it was called for them.

Since they had been to the club themselves it had changed its venue; it still carried the same name, but now its home was in a disused working men's club just around the corner from where Tim lived as a boy and where his mum still lived.

Would Tim tell her he had a booking there? He wasn't sure, she knew that club as it used to be, but did she know of the change and the local gossip … ?

Arriving for the given time, Tim and Alf made their entrance, the former seeking the guy he had spoken to and Alf taking care of the costume especially made for the evening; wacky as ever, a very short black and white fur coat, knee length boots, white stockings and the hat! A huge, bold paper lampshade, complete with an orange bulb inside which flashed on and of like a Belisha beacon!

The guys were super welcoming, making sure the lighting was absolutely correct and knowing when to put the room Into darkness for effect – and what an effect, they got it just right. It was an evening to be remembered and enjoyed by the guys and "girls."

## Even for "The Star of the Show" the Wait Becomes Too Much

So you see, out of persuasion came success. Tim never thought he'd be a part of something like that, but perhaps the other story that should be told is the one where the owner of another club wasn't quite sure about the timing of the show and despite many requests from Tim kept saying, "half an hour lads, half an hour." In the end it got too much, the 'star' got nervous and had Alf looking for an escape route.

Alf came back and said the only way out is the fire escape! "That will do!" came the reply … so there was the supposed star of the evening, climbing down the metal fire escape in 'her' orange fur costume, with all the guys wishing her "Goodnight Mrs … mind how you go!" If only they had known …

A few miles on the journey home, a police car pulled up alongside at some traffic lights … the look on the guy's face said it all, as the police officer smiled and winked at the old girl in the car! So you see, it's kind of fun, dressing up and then coming back to yourself to remember.

There was the fun, the satisfaction of giving so much pleasure, but never a thought of this being a part of his life. As soon as the lights went down and the curtains closed, the wigs were back in their boxes, the makeup all packed away; it was forgotten and they were blokes again, using the gents' toilets as before.


## Saying Goodbye to the Florist's Shops

Like many people, Tim & Alf were proud of what they achieved over their many years together since they first met after walking back from the bank, but because of Tim's ill health they had to give up the shops. There were no financial problems, and they supported each other in all things, even the decision to walk away from the very successful business they had created from scratch, to become the first choice when one was looking for that special bouquet or floral tribute; Tim's reputation and expertise were well known, and not just locally.


## Freedom to Travel and Moving Home

The pain of seeing the shops close, within 24 hours, required a unique bond created between Tim & Alf, and they viewed the situation as "every cloud has a silver lining." As time went by, the last dog having passed away and with no florist's shops to manage, the change in circumstances enabled Tim & Alf to have many enjoyable holidays abroad, exploring North Africa, Goa, and even further afar.

Life continued to improve, as they were also able to move away from the two people who had given them so much grief over so many years … yes, the homophobic neighbours!

## UK Law May Have Changed, But Not So in Many Countries

One of the many holidays he and Alf had been fortunate to be able to go on, for it is probably worth mentioning here, was the previously mentioned holiday in Morocco. Tim was sitting on a doorstep of a hotel in the Main Street when he was approached by a tall, good-looking young man who asked why he was sitting where he was. Tim said that his partner had gone back into the hotel to retrieve something from their room. Because of health conditions, Tim was sitting down to wait.

Tim was shocked to hear the young man declare he was a police officer, and sitting alone, as Tim was, gave reason for him to think Tim was offering sex. He could easily have been arrested, but upon producing medication the guy walked on. One winces to think that all happened in the year 2004, more than 37 years after the change to the Sexual Offences Act 1967.

# CHAPTER 8

# 2000s: The Law Change

## Marriage Act 2006 ... Again, UK One of the First Countries

The Marriage Act that came circa 2006 made so much more possible. True, it didn't stop the possibility of the dreaded AIDS; simply put, it made the people more careful as in all partnerships, heterosexual or homosexual.

The Marriage Act also gave freedom never known. The younger generation in particular were excited by the fact that they, too, could be married, like their friends and family members, even though they were openly gay, but one only has to look at statistics ... they were only married for such a short time before they needed change in their lives. A sad reflection of the times maybe, but as the previous pages have shown, there's more to life than sex. As life, in all its glory shows, be you heterosexual or homosexual, times change, but hope goes on for us all.

Some, perhaps including us, are waiting for the knight in shining armour to arrive and never give up; that in itself is part of God's plan. Some are lucky, perhaps, but there have to be disappointments. It's that excitement that humans beg, crave, and live by. Hope is the greatest gift. Hope of that kind is so special in our lives.

Reflecting as we must in this book, we wish so much that it was possible for us to change some of the things around us. We know that's possible, if we can only bring to the fore the mistakes that are made.

Only recently a celebrity married his partner; life was apparently good for them, for a while, but then the relationship fell apart. Marriage, the ambiance of being a 'celebrity' means nothing if it does not contain a genuine love, a love that is not based on the material wealth of life.

# Marriage Act 2006 – "Life Changing"

Aware of the difficult times people who were gay had had with the passing of a loved one, one family saying everything belonged to their son etc., when the Marriage Act 2006 became law Tim and Alf decided to become Civil Partners. By now they had been together 36 years! Even the Superintendent Registrar insisted on taking the ceremony. She had never heard of two people being together that many years before making it official, she said. Family and friends gathered for the occasion and a garden party afterwards.

Sadly, reflecting on the trend since, at least, the start of the 21$^{st}$ century, how many couples, heterosexual or homosexual, will be celebrating their 36$^{h}$ anniversary in years to come? … Even more concerning, how many couples will survive more than 10 years together? A sign of the times, for better or for worse.


# Gay Relationships Do Last

Perhaps it was the right time in many ways; if nothing else they had proved the doubters wrong – it has lasted and will continue to do so. Tim and Alf were, if nothing else, growing older, and health problems were not passing them by. Family and friends were kind and only 12 months ago, Tim's family gave a party to celebrate 50 years of Tim and Alf being together. So you see, gay relationships can, do, and will continue to last. It is not all frivolity, etc.

However, it is felt to record the entire 50 years here would be both laborious and no doubt boring to the reader, as would it be for anyone writing about that length of time in most people's lives – unless they had done something spectacular.

# 50 Years Together – Is There a Secret Ingredient?

Tim and Alf say they have had a good partnership, sharing every stage together and making decisions together. It can't be a sharing relationship if responsibilities are placed on one person. They felt they were lucky from the start, in as much as their families had accepted them both for who they were. The subject of gayness was never discussed, they were simply two people in a good relationship. There was never any thought of one being more special than the other, as with any heterosexual couple's troubles when a 'mummy' thinks her child is the more important.

Tim and Alf always have been, and remain so in these latter years, a couple, and wherever they have travelled have been treated as such.

Easy? No, of course it isn't easy, especially when you're younger and each have their own ideas and opinions; you have to learn the art of living together before anything. They found each other after all those years ago, made promises and have lived by them.

# Marriage Act 2006 – Very Broad and Widely Impacting

To continue talking about the Marriage Act 2006, a subject which caused much discussion in many areas for many years; unlike the act concerning death and funerals, which had rarely been changed, it was known the "Act" that covers all details regarding two people being married legally. The service, or ceremony, as some prefer to call it, must take place before an authorised person – not necessarily a clergyman. It can be a registrar, superintendent or deputy, or any person holding the required certificate entitling them to carry out the ceremony with the required dignity. This, of course, was for two people of the opposite sex, a 'normal' marriage in other words.

It was always known that others, homosexuals for instance, would have wanted this. It was a dream to be officially recognised as a couple, but the bigots fought against the law change for many years.

Of course, pre the 2006 Marriage Act becoming law, there were difficulties in all areas; to name the obvious: Mortgages, where two people wanted to buy a home – this had to be done in one name only and one can imagine … difficulties when one of the partners passed away. Utility services were also engaged under one owner, one name; the list goes on.

But in 2006 this act of parliament was finally entitling same-sex people to enter into what was known as a Civil Partnership. This was the answer to so many problems: it legalized the partnership, it covered the tax requirements, and it gave the gays a reason to be proud of who they are.

Celebrities and the like, sportsmen and women etc., jumped to be the first, as well as ordinary guys and girls. However, although it was an official ceremony, it was not a marriage and, as well as not being able to have the full wedding etc. in church, it fell short of what many wanted.


## 2006 Marriage Act – Meaning Full Exclusions?

Like others Tim had friends who were disappointed that they had spent so much money on something that was not what they thought it was. The legality to be able to enter into a legal & binding 'partnership' was sufficient for many, because it put the relationship on a firm footing and opened up so many doors, but even to this day there are many who wish to be, 'properly' married, as they call it. As referenced above, Tim and Alf entered their civil partnership in 2006 and have been contented with this arrangement ever since.

If nothing else in this world matters, we should give thanks to our brothers and sisters who suffered so horrendously so that we could wear a ring on our finger with pride and not have to suffer the indignities of pointing fingers.

## Accepting Advice in the Spirit It Is Given

Being older has many benefits; we have seen so many things on life's highway change. True, some for good, some for no other reason than to create problems. Like many before him, Tim has witnessed the discerning look and the twitching eyebrow when the words "I remember" are uttered, usually in good faith.

But as you will have read, there have been many things that have changed in the homosexual world over many years. If you are discovering this pathway, take time to enjoy the escapades, the daring and the never ending love that has been part of this book, but don't ignore, because you think you know better, the drama, the truths, and the advice offered.

… To put it simply, and bluntly, any "silly little bitch" can go out and camp it up, swearing and drawing attention, but Tim's key advice, and the only one that matters, is to conduct yourself nicely, check and make sure that you are a male, and not a little girl, whatever you think you want to be. Be proud, and in years to come, you will be glad you're not a 70-year-old man talking like a little girl. Keep a watch for the public grimaces of people in the street when they hear that! … But most of all, remember your "brothers and sisters" who would have given the world to be in your shoes and share your privileges._

## "Coming Out" No Longer a Taboo Subject

In a list of chapters and paragraphs contained herein, the writer has endeavoured to include words, phrases, etc. used by the gay community (See appendix 2 for a summary list). Over the years, few seem to have changed to any greater degree, but speak to the man or woman in the street and they will be familiar with the expression "coming out." Perhaps it is one of those things that has become fashionable; certainly Tim would admit he can never remember "coming out," it just wasn't done. Not to say that gays of the day would have been ignorant to its meaning, simply that it wasn't done, nor accepted by society pre-1970s, or even later.

Like all things associated to the subject, the popularity of the words is associated with the freedom brought about by the law of 1967 and of course the modern generation.

## "Coming Out" in Its Purest Definition – Is It Necessary? Is It Beneficial?

"Coming out" to friends, family etc. almost seems like an admission to being different, and if you are, so what? … You are simply putting a label on yourself, and who needs that.

The quieter, more reserved folk prefer to keep some things private, and you know if you look into the right areas it's usually the folk who don't need to who make a song and dance about the issue, who do the most shouting, and when they have made the grand display announcement are surprised when the general reaction is, "Well, everyone knew anyway, or at least we guessed!"

The younger reader will probably say they're just being themselves, being loud; remember, if you will, our brave brothers of the past. They didn't need to, they didn't want to, they had their own aura and they kept themselves a mystery, and how successful they were. Many of the gays of today, but with a little more experience behind them, have held good jobs in all sorts of environments, in all walks of life, not to mention the traveling and mixing in all kinds of gatherings, and being aware of the nudges and glances which said "Are they?" or, "Do you think they're a couple?" There's many a look that says you are; take for instance the old, yes, very old, "My parents don't know" … Who do they think they're kidding?

There was, and is, a segment of society who shared no embarrassment being who they were, and is fair to say "why shouldn't they?"

The majority of homosexuals have, and continue to, always acted with decency and decorum, never wanting to advertise the fact. You are who you are, yes … people can assume, but as long as you conduct yourself properly you can be who you want, and who you are! Why should you announce the fact you are gay? … So what if you are … do heterosexuals 'advertise' they are 'straight'?

Maybe, through the ages, musicians and the like have been known to be a little more flamboyant than the rest of us and have gone from one style to another, the change in dress, to music, and in general the presentation of themselves and their music.

Possibly the changes in and around the 60s had a greater impact on society when we lived in the hippie era. From the elegance of dinner suits and evening gowns in which they graced the stage to perform, to the youngsters since, who are being brought to entertain us wearing entirely different garb.

No longer was it thought to dress properly; the more casual and carefree they seemed, the better it seemed to fit their style of music. They were out to attract the younger, impressionable girls of the day with their tight trousers, but, it seemed, the young males too! Even older men were keen to join in the modern look, regardless of whether it suited them or not, and in turn attracted the young males too!

It was as if history was repeating itself, the days when men wore no underwear; to some it was sexy, to others simply an attraction unwanted, but perhaps it's true that fashion always has a place.

Men of all ages were attracted to what was on display, whether they were gay or not, and so it became natural for young men, boys, youths to dress in that way, and many 'stars', 'celebrities', call them what you will, gained a notoriety for being interested in more than would have been admitted in previous years.

Now, in more recent times, these are the people who shouted, "I've come out," "I should never have got married, I did it because it seemed more respectable and the fans expected it of me!" … What rubbish! One, maybe two, sometimes three marriages behind them and goodness only knows what stresses have been caused simply because they couldn't admit who they were. The happy phrase is the one that says, "Coming out … I've never been *in,* dear."

## It's Reality!

For many nothing has changed; it seems over the many years being queer, gay, homosexual, "batting for the other side," whichever way you put it, the reality is solid now and remains part of creation.

"No picking or choosing," is an old saying, and means exactly what it says; we are what we are, God's children and just a small part of His entire creation, and it is for that reason that this book is written – in the hope it may help at least one confused soul.

It isn't meant to show you the way through this somewhat difficult path, how to behave, how to dress, how to anything – we're all different. We all make a few mistakes here and there along the way, mistakes of many kinds.

# CHAPTER 9

# 2020s: Daily Life Changed – Forever?

## Technology and Social Media

It can't be forgotten in these changing times that Tim, as a lad, was used to playing in the streets, not shut away in his room with technology, and seeing the world at its rawest. That was part of growing up; learning the fundamentals of life, learning how to create entertainment, learning new skills, all influenced by one's parents, family, the local community & surroundings, totally content with what life had handed down to Tim and (like all children of Tim's generation) totally unaware there is a big world outside of the UK, or even outside of one's home town.

This new world, where everything is conducted 'online', from obtaining the latest news and social chit chat/messaging through to seeking relationships, is creating an environment where there are no geographical barriers. Anyone, anywhere in the world can be connected, just as if all parties are in the same location.

## One World – As It's Global

Today this single 'global' environment has become the norm, driven by the advances in technology that now intrude into the way each and every one of us conducts ourselves in performing our daily tasks (or are expected to, potentially leaving many who were born pre-Generation X feeling totally lost).

Tim thinks back to his teenage years, which for the biggest part were in wartime, when in local places were billeted prisoners of war from around the world and servicemen from other countries walking around in freedom. For many locals, this was the first time interacting with human beings from outside of the UK.

Every so often, a young lady from the area where they lived could be seen walking alongside one of the locally billeted guys, as males and females have always done; but occasionally the guy, usually from America, would be of a darker skin colour. Now, that wasn't to be seen and drew many comments from neighbours and the like. The remarks are not printable here, or elsewhere, but as it happened, Tim himself experienced such a mixed-race family, as two of his cousins married visiting American service-men, and went on to have a wonderful life and family in America.

Today we have multiracial communities across the world and that does not exclude the gay community's mixed-race couples, all of whom now have the benefit of being able to keep in touch and visit thanks to the developments in technology, both in terms of aviation and mobile communication/social media.


## An Afternoon Reflecting on Memories Comes to an End

After several coffees and a large portion of apple and blackberry crumble, with custard (of course!), Tim lost all track of time and started his journey back home after a very reflective few hours.

Tim's thoughts walking home were very mixed. Many happy memories, content with how society has opened up to accepting homosexuality/same sex partnerships/marriages. However, Tim kept thinking about the two young guys walking hand in hand earlier, clearly telling the world they were gay. Was this accept-able ? ... Was it showing disrespect for fundamental "expected" human conduct when in public? Or is their behaviour the new norm? For those born pre-Generation Y (Echo Boomers, also referred to as Millennials), and even more so for the likes of Tim & Alf (being part of the first Baby Boomer era), having to ac-cept the impact, and one may say the benefit of, the various law changes (1967, & 2006, 2014) that enable same sex couples to be and act no different to any other 'segment' of society. There is also the influence of 'advances' (?) in technology on the way we live our lives, with whom we live them, regardless of race/religion and where we live.

## But Has the Pendulum Swung Too Far?

This is a subject Tim found himself engaged in discussing with his nephews and their children during the next family get together. However, the discussion quickly widened to encompass many other changes that had occurred over the generations due to the impact of innovation, advances in technology, religion, demographic profiles, cultural mix, climate change, food sustainability etc., with the one question remaining unanswered: are all the changes for the betterment of society, or has the pendulum of change swung too far?

# CHAPTER 10

# Beyond 2021: An Opportunity to Recalibrate?

## Generation Alpha – Impact of Technology – Social Media

Tim & Alf's great-nieces and nephews, being born during the Generation X era, are certainly experiencing a different life style to that of Tim and Alf (The first Baby Boomer generation), and even that experienced during their parents' time, of completing their studies, starting to earn an income, finding a partner, and starting a family.

But what will the world, and life, comprise of for Tim and Alf's great nieces and nephews' children? By 2025, which is the year when the youngest Alphas are born, Generation Alpha will account to 2 billion of the global population. Generation Alpha is considered to be the most technological-infused demographic up to date. They are the first generation entirely born within the 21st century. They are also known as the iGeneration, as they use smartphones and tablets naturally. These children were born along with iPhones, iPads, and mobile phone applications. They don't know or can't imagine how life was without them.

They are not afraid of technology or touching buttons to learn what those buttons do. Alphas learn by doing.

Generation Alpha is growing up with the familiar voice of Siri, Alexa, and Google Assistant in their home.

In the world of the Alphas, interacting with artificial intelligence and voice assistants is simply natural.

The power and influence of social media appears to increase exponentially as each day passes. Reflecting upon two subjects, in particular, clearly demonstrates this power.

1. Sexual Abuse of Females – The "Me Too" movement
2. The woke brigade, who campaign to remove any distinction between
   - Man – Woman
   - Father – Mother
   - Whether a child is born male or female

Just to name a few examples of how everything must be 'politically correct.'

Would the growth/influence, not just in one country but globally, ever have happened if the world of connectivity, the internet and social media never existed?

So much change from what Tim and Alf have taken for granted and been totally accustomed to for more than 70 years: watching the BBC/ITV on the television, using the landline to make phone calls, reading the daily newspaper, wearing a suit and tie, showing respect, receiving respect from those younger, never declaring their love for each other outside of their home, etc.

## What Will Life Be Like Come 2050, Or Even By 2030?

The Generation Alpha, and generations thereafter, find themselves in a totally new environment driven by technology, whether it be simply communication via social media and receiving news alerts on mobile devices, or one's health being monitored & diagnosed remotely, however … will the one fundamental of human life that has been in existence since time immemorial – the need to love and be loved, to share life's experiences together – also change?

# Everything Changing for the Best?

Books, particularly this one, are not written, printed, and published in days, weeks, etc.; so, as a conclusion, it is worth noting at this final stage (and as the basis of this book is history) that on 20th December 2021 the British Government announced that a bill had been passed declaring that a pardon is to be granted to all gay men & women who have been arrested/charged with acts concerning homosexuality over more recent years. This is certainly a step in the right direction for so many, who came into this category because of simple acts and were pounced upon by local police, their character besmirched all in the name of …?

It was said earlier in the book that laws changed in 1967, but it seems strange that not everything changed for the best and even today, many decent guys live their lives wondering and worrying if someone, somewhere, will find out their secret and ask the question:

It's a Sin … ?
All in the Name of Love!

Only YOU can decide!

# Appendix 1 – Demographic Cohort

| Society Labels Assigned to each Generation – Demographic Cohort | |
|---|---|
| **Alpha or iGeneration**<br><br>The first generation entirely born within the 21st century. Also known as the iGeneration. The children of the Millennials. | Born: 2013–2025<br>Coming of Age: 2031–2043 |
| **Generation Z**<br><br>Gen Z kids will grow up with a highly sophisticated media and computer environment and will be more Internet savvy and expert than their Gen Y forerunners. | Born: 1995–2012<br>Coming of Age: 2013–2020 |
| **Generation Y, Echo Boomers or Millenniums**<br><br>Gen Y kids often raised in dual income or single parent families have been more involved in family purchases … everything from groceries to new cars. One in nine Gen Yers has a credit card co-signed by a parent. | Born: 1977–1994<br>Coming of Age: 1998-2006 |

| **Generation X or "The Lost "Generation** | Born: 1966–1976<br>Coming of Age:<br>1988–1994 |
| --- | --- |
| Gen X is often characterized by high levels of skepticism, "what's in it for me" attitudes and a reputation for some of the worst music to ever gain popularity. Now, moving into adulthood William Morrow (Generations) cited the childhood divorce of many Gen Xers as "one of the most decisive experiences influencing how Gen Xers will shape their own families". | |
| **Boomers II or Generation Jones** | Born: 1955–1965<br>Coming of Age:<br>1973–1983 |
| This first post-Watergate generation lost much of its trust in government and optimistic views the Boomers I maintained. Economic struggles including the oil embargo of 1979 reinforced a sense of "I'm out for me" and narcissism and a focus on self-help and skepticism over media and institutions is representative of attitudes of this cohort. | |

| **Boomers I or The Baby Boomers**<br><br>The first Boomer segment is bounded by the Kennedy and Martin Luther King assassinations, the Civil Rights movements and the Vietnam War. | Born: 1946–1954<br>Coming of Age: 1963–1972 |
| --- | --- |
| **Post-War Cohort**<br><br>This generation had significant opportunities in jobs and education as the War ended and a post-war economic boom struck. However, the growth in Cold War tensions, the potential for nuclear war and other never before seen threats led to levels of discomfort and uncertainty throughout the generation. Members of this group value security, comfort, and familiar, known activities and environments. | Born: 1928–1945<br>Coming of Age: 1946–1963 |
| **World War II**<br><br>People in this cohort shared in a common goal of defeating the Axis powers. There was an accepted sense of "deferment" among this group, contrasted with the emphasis on "me" in more recent (i.e. Gen X) cohorts. | Born: 1922 to 1927<br>Coming of Age: 1940–1945 |

| **The Depression Era**<br><br>Depression era individuals tend to be conservative, compulsive savers, maintain low debt and use more secure financial products like CDs versus stocks. These individuals tend to feel a responsibility to leave a legacy to their children. Tend to be patriotic, oriented toward work before pleasure, respect for authority, have a sense of moral obligation. | Born: 1912–1921<br>Coming of Age: 1930–1939 |
| --- | --- |

# Appendix 2 – Glossary – Gay Language/Terms

| | |
|---|---|
| Bat for the Other Side | A person who is gay |
| Camp | Acting effeminate |
| Chickens | Young gay males |
| Coming Out | Being open with family, friends regarding one's sexuality |
| Cottage | Male Toilet |
| Cruising | Looking for hook up with a gay guy |
| Dandies | |
| Dorothy's Friend | Male who is gay |
| Drag | Male Dressing up in female clothes |
| Dyke | Name used to describe a female who is gay |
| Faggot | Slang/derogatory expression used by heterosexual males to describe a male who is gay |
| Fag Hag | Female who prefers the company of gay guys |
| Family | Someone who is also gay |
| Fish | Heterosexual Female |

| | |
|---|---|
| Gaydar | 6th sense used by gay guys to identify a guy who is gay<br><br>A unique ability for a gay person to recognise the body language of an other gay person |
| Ginger | Slag for being gay/acting as if gay |
| Mincing along | A male who walks swinging his hips etc., acting like a female |
| Mollie Houses | A meeting place for gay guys |
| Queen | The partner who takes the female role in a gay relationship<br><br>Also can be used to describe an older gay person |

# Appendix 3 – References

**1967 Sexual Offences Act**
https://www.parliament.uk/about/living-heritage/
transformingsociety/private-lives/relationships/collections1/
sexual-offences-act-1967/sexual-offences-act-1967/

**2006 Civil Partnership Act becomes law**
https://www.legislation.gov.uk/ukpga/2004/33/contents

**2014 Same Sex Marriage Becomes law**
Same sex marriage becomes law – GOV.UK (www.gov.uk)

**Generation Alpha, also called the iGeneration, is the
most influential generation of the 21st century and here
is why**
https://interestingengineering.com/generation-alpha-the-
children-of-the-millennial#:~:text=Generation%20Alpha%20
is%20considered%20to%20be%20the%20most,century.%20
They%20are%20also%20known%20as%20the%20iGeneration.

# Rate this book on our website!

www.novum-publishing.co.uk

# The author

Born in 1934, Jonathan E. is a retired florist from Birmingham. Now 87 years old, Jonathan was the second youngest of seven children and has remained a bachelor. He served two years of National Service in the Far East, achieving a promotion, and enjoys gardening, baking, and home decorating.

# The publisher

*He who stops
getting better
stops being good.*

This is the motto of novum publishing, and our focus
is on finding new manuscripts, publishing them and
offering long-term support to the authors.
Our publishing house was founded in 1997, and since
then it has become THE expert for new authors and
has won numerous awards.

**Our editorial team will peruse each manuscript
within a few weeks free of charge and without
obligation.**

You will find more information about
novum publishing and our books on the internet:

w w w . n o v u m - p u b l i s h i n g . c o . u k